Contents

1. The Intersection of Zen, Archery, and Coding: A Journey Begins 5

2. Embracing the Emacs Environment 6
   2.1. Understanding Emacs Philosophy 6
   2.2. Setting Up Your Emacs Workspace 8
   2.3. Navigating the Emacs Interface 11
   2.4. Extending Emacs Functionality 14
   2.5. Customizing Emacs Keybindings 17

3. The Zen Art of Focus 21
   3.1. The Breath of Code 21
   3.2. Managing Mindful Work Sessions 23
   3.3. Creating a Zen-Inducing Environment 26
   3.4. Cultivating Discipline in Code 28
   3.5. The Balance of Form and Function 31

4. Archery Techniques Applied to Coding 35
   4.1. The Zen Archer's Posture 35
   4.2. Setting Targets and Goals 37
   4.3. The Release: Letting Go of Perfectionism 40
   4.4. Adapting to Change: The Archer's Way 42
   4.5. The Follow-through in Coding 45

5. Mastering Emacs Skills 48
   5.1. Essential Emacs Commands 48
   5.2. The Power of Macros 50
   5.3. Exploring Emacs Modes 53
   5.4. Debugging with Precision 56
   5.5. Version Control Integration 58

6. The Zen Coding Techniques 62
   6.1. Coding with Mindfulness 62
   6.2. Zen in Error Handling 64
   6.3. The Art of Code Review 66
   6.4. Refactoring: The Zen Way 70
   6.5. Continuous Learning and Adaptation 72

7. Creating an Emacs Workflow 76
   7.1. Workflow Foundations 76
   7.2. The Role of Scheduling in Coding 78
   7.3. Streamlining Tasks and Projects 81
   7.4. Enhancing Workflow with Plugins 84
   7.5. Reviewing and Improving Your Workflow 86

8. Zen and the Art of Coding Under Pressure 89

8.1. Keeping Calm in Code Crises 89

8.2. From Pressure to Progress 91

8.3. Effective Communication Under Stress 94

8.4. Mindful Time Management 96

8.5. The Zen of Post-Deadline Reflection 99

9. Integrating Emacs into the Professional Environment 102

9.1. Deploying Emacs in Team Projects 102

9.2. Collaborative Coding in Emacs 104

9.3. Emacs for Remote Work 107

9.4. Interviewing with Emacs Skills 109

9.5. Professional Growth with Emacs Mastery 111

10. The Philosophical Core: Zen and Mastery 115

10.1. The Role of Zen in Mastery 115

10.2. Mastery as a Lifelong Journey 117

10.3. The Intersection of Art and Technology 119

10.4. Finding Purpose in Coding 121

10.5. Connecting with Community 123

11. Maintaining a Zen Edge in a Fast-Paced World 127

11.1. Staying Grounded Amidst Distractions 127

11.2. The Art of Slow Coding 129

11.3. Preventing Burnout 132

11.4. Balancing Professional and Personal Life 134

11.5. Embracing Change with Grace 137

12. Exploring Advanced Emacs Techniques 140

12.1. Harnessing Advanced Commands 140

12.2. Mastering Emacs Lisp 142

12.3. Leveraging External Tools 146

12.4. Advanced Debugging Techniques 148

12.5. Optimization for Performance 151

13. Global Perspectives: Zen and Technology 155

13.1. Zen's Influence on Global Technology Cultures 155

13.2. The Rise of Mindfulness in Tech 157

13.3. Case Studies in Zen-Centric Development 159

13.4. Cultivating Global Tech Communities 161

13.5. Building a Zen Future in Technology 164

14. The Spiritual Journey of a Zen Coder 167

14.1. The Internal Landscape of Zen Coding 167

14.2. Transcending Technical Boundaries 169

14.3. The Zen Path to Code Simplicity 172

14.4. The Role of Compassion in Coding 174

14.5. A Lifelong Commitment to Learning 176

15. Reflections on The Zen Archer's Emacs 180

15.1. Revisiting the Connection Between Zen and Emacs 180

15.2. Lessons Learned from the Zen Archer 182

15.3. Crafting Your Personal Zen Coding Philosophy 185

15.4. Preparing for Future Coding Journeys 187

15.5. Celebrating Your Achievements 190

"In the pursuit of understanding, one must become the arrow, fluid yet purposeful, to navigate the complexities of change."

— Bruce Lee

1. The Intersection of Zen, Archery, and Coding: A Journey Begins

Zen is often associated with the meditative practices that help one achieve a heightened state of awareness and peaceful mindfulness. Archery, meanwhile, requires focus, an intimate knowledge of the bow, and the ability to hit a target with accuracy. Coding with Emacs is surprisingly similar. While seemingly disparate, these disciplines share common principles that, when combined, create a transformative journey into efficient and mindful coding practices. By absorbing the spirit of the Zen archer, we can learn to navigate the Emacs environment with skill and precision, achieving a seamless integration of thought and execution.

This book, "The Zen Archer's Emacs: Hit the Bullseye with Each Coding Shot," invites you to blend ancient wisdom with modern technology, unraveling the mysteries of coding in Emacs to become more than just a proficient coder, but a Zen master of your craft. Whether you're a seasoned Emacs user or completely new to it, the lessons within these pages promise to enrich both your coding skills and your personal growth.

As we embark on this journey, we'll explore the rules of engagement — where discipline and intuition go hand in hand — guiding you through the coding labyrinth with the precision of an archer's arrow. It's not just about hitting the target; it's about understanding the journey of the arrow to the bullseye. Welcome to a new perspective on coding.

2. Embracing the Emacs Environment

2.1. Understanding Emacs Philosophy

Emacs is not merely a text editor; it stands as a testament to a unique philosophy that champions the ideals of freedom, customization, and extensibility. This philosophy fundamentally shapes how users interact with and leverage Emacs within their coding practices. To truly understand Emacs, one must delve into its core principles, drawing parallels to the virtues found in Zen and archery.

At the heart of Emacs's philosophy is the notion that your working environment should be adaptable to your personal coding style rather than fitting a predetermined mold. Much like a Zen archer who tailors their approach based on their strengths and weaknesses, Emacs invites its users to hone their individual tools and processes for maximum effectiveness. The fundamental belief here is that the tools of coding should not dictate your workflow; rather, you cultivate and shape those tools to serve your needs. This acts as an essential springboard for mindfulness in coding, where each keystroke, command, or macro is a deliberate act of creation tailored to achieve the highest level of clarity and focus.

Extensibility stands as another pillar of Emacs's philosophy. The text editor is designed to grow with you, accommodating new paradigms and techniques over time. Just as an archer practices integrating different techniques to adapt to various targets and conditions, programmers can expand the capabilities of Emacs through its vast ecosystem of packages and extensions. This allows for a highly personalized programming experience that reflects the user's unique skill set and preferences. Users can implement new programming languages, customization options, and keybindings easily, further enhancing their efficiency and productivity within the Emacs environment.

Freedom is pivotal in the Emacs philosophy, reminiscent of the Zen principle of liberation from restraint. This freedom manifests in several ways, one of the most significant being the freedom to modify the code itself. Written in Emacs Lisp, users are encouraged to explore the inner workings of their editor, enabling them to make bespoke changes that resonate with their specific needs and ideologies. This aligns with the practice of mindfulness; every customization is an opportunity for reflection and self-awareness, ensuring that the tools you use align with your goals and values as a coder.

Furthermore, the connection between Zen principles and Emacs strengthens the user's understanding of coding as an art form. Just as an archer aims for precision and grace in their movement, coders can approach their work as an expression of creativity, refining their art with each iteration. The intertwining of Zen philosophy with Emacs leads to a more intentional coding practice, one that emphasizes patience, focus, and steady improvement. As you engage with Emacs, strive to embody the disciplined mind of a practitioner seeking improvement and mastery rather than merely looking to complete tasks.

In this spirit, the process of coding in Emacs transcends mere technical proficiency. It becomes a holistic experience aiming not just at producing functional software but also at fostering personal growth and deepening understanding. Learning Emacs is akin to practicing archery: it requires the same dedication and commitment to honing one's skills. Each frustration or moment of confusion can be seen as an opportunity for mindfulness and reflection in practice. By embracing the philosophy of Emacs, you're not simply aiming to hit the proverbial coding bullseye but cultivating a deeper relationship with the practice of programming itself.

Finally, incorporating the concept of "community" into the Emacs philosophy is essential. Just as Zen communities provide support and encouragement along the path of personal development, the Emacs community embodies collaboration and shared knowledge. Engaging with this community through forums and discussions enriches your coding journey, allowing for the exchange of insights and techniques that can deepen your understanding and mastery of both primary coding principles and the Emacs environment.

In conclusion, the Emacs philosophy serves as a foundational guide through which coders can navigate their technical journey. By embracing the spirit of adaptability and personal growth, much like the path of a Zen archer, you can transform not only your coding practices but also your relationship with technology. It is an invitation to view coding not just as an obligation but as a profound journey into the essence of creation, mastery, and enlightenment. With an appreciation for these principles, you will unlock the true potential of Emacs, allowing for an enriched experience that both empowers your coding journey and fosters your personal growth.

2.2. Setting Up Your Emacs Workspace

A well-organized Emacs workspace is essential for achieving efficiency and fostering a productive coding environment. When setting up your Emacs workspace, think of it as crafting your own archery range—each element is carefully placed to enhance your focus, accuracy, and comfort. This process is about more than just installing software; it's a transformation of your coding experience into a Zen-like practice that allows for mindful engagement with your work.

Begin by downloading the latest version of Emacs from the official website. The installation process may vary slightly depending on your operating system, but the essential principles of customization are universally applicable. For those using Linux, you may find Emacs available in your distribution's repositories, which often simplifies the process with package managers like APT for Debian-based systems or YUM for Red Hat-based ones. MacOS users can leverage Homebrew for an elegant installation, while Windows users can utilize the precompiled binaries provided on the Emacs website. Regardless of the platform, the goal is to ensure that you have a base installation ready to be tailored to your needs.

Once you have Emacs installed, the next step is to create the configuration file, init.el or .emacs in your home directory. This file is your canvas for customization, akin to an archer preparing their bow for precision shots. By entering your preferences, keybindings, and packages, you lay the foundation for a workspace that reflects your unique coding style and enhances your focus.

In this configuration file, start by defining key settings such as font size and theme. Select a font that minimizes strain on your eyes during long coding sessions—monospaced fonts like Source Code Pro or Fira Code not only promote clarity but can be aesthetically pleasing as well, drawing parallels to the beauty found in archery. Themes, on the other hand, can greatly influence your emotional state as you code. Opt for softer, tranquil colors or a classic, darker theme that reduces glare. Packages like doom-themes or gruvbox-theme can transform the visual landscape of your Emacs environment, creating a serene backdrop that supports your coding practice.

After establishing visual elements, turn your attention to the functionality that will streamline your workflow. Emacs is vast, but diving into the package management system effectively can elevate your experience from basic text editing to a powerful coding powerhouse. The package manager use-package can simplify the process of installing and configuring external packages. With an elegant syntax, it allows you to wrap your package declarations neatly, enabling you to load them only when needed, which contributes to a snappier startup time.

Consider essential packages like company-mode for autocompletion, simplifying syntax as you code. This mirrors the role of an advanced sight for an archer—giving you clearer options while removing mental clutter. For those who work with code repositories, integrating magit as a powerful Git interface into your Emacs setup can transform how you view and manage version control. Time spent navigating Git commands can be reduced to simple keystrokes, enhancing focus and allowing you to concentrate on the task at hand.

Another highly recommended package is org-mode, which offers an unparalleled system for organizing your notes, tasks, and projects. There's a Zen-like quality in how it helps you sort your thoughts. Utilizing org-capture makes it simple to document ideas or tasks as they arise, while `org-agenda` can help manage your time effectively, allowing you to calendar your coding sprints with clarity and purpose, ensuring you neither overextend nor neglect essential breaks to maintain mindfulness.

As with archery, the setup of your workspace should involve mindfulness and careful adjustments based on your experiences. After this initial configuration, it's wise to constantly reflect on what works for you and what could be optimized further. This iterative process is crucial. Should you find that a specific package slows you down or distracts more than it aids, don't hesitate to disable or replace it. Similarly, as an archer practices regularly to refine their aim, allow yourself the grace of regularly revisiting your setup and infusing new tools or strategies as you evolve in your coding journeys.

Managing your buffers—each open file or project—ensures that your workspace remains uncluttered, much like an archer's stance should be free of extraneous movements. Use built-in commands like `winner-mode` for window management. It allows you to undo window configurations, helping you revert if you feel your workspace has become chaotic.

Additionally, consider delving into the integration of version control, using packages like `vc`, which comes prepackaged with Emacs. This will encourage you to work mindfully while keeping track of your progress without requiring you to constantly switch contexts.

Lastly, do not overlook the power of keyboard shortcuts. Just as an archer's movements become second nature through practice, Emacs commands can be memorized and embodied through frequent use. Regularly practicing key combinations will enhance your fluency in navigating your workspace, reducing mental friction and ensuring that you can flow seamlessly between tasks.

Setting up your Emacs workspace is an ongoing journey toward achieving a coding practice that feels both intuitive and fulfilling. Much like the dedication required in archery, approach it with an open mind, ready to adapt and mold your environment into one that nourishes your focus and aligns with your goals. The process involves self-exploration, frequent reflection, and iterative improvement, allowing your workspace to transform into a sanctuary of productivity —where each line of code is a precise shot aimed toward the target of your coding aspirations.

2.3. Navigating the Emacs Interface

In navigating the Emacs interface, you will embark on a journey similar to that of a Zen archer stepping onto the shooting range. Each component of Emacs is meticulously crafted to facilitate your flow, enhancing your focus and creativity as you write and edit code. In this section, we will explore the various elements of the Emacs interface, ensuring that your experience is both seamless and productive as you transition from concept to execution.

To begin with, let's explore the layout of the Emacs environment itself. The Emacs interface is composed of several key parts: the buffer, the minibuffer, the menu bar, and various modes. Understanding these components is akin to grasping the elements of your bow and arrow. Each part has its designated purpose, and learning to maneuver between them efficiently will elevate your coding experience.

The buffer is the main workspace in Emacs, where you write, edit, and interact with your code. Each buffer represents a distinct document or file, and you can open multiple buffers simultaneously. Think of these buffers as individual targets on the range—each one demands your attention and precision. You can switch between buffers using the command C-x b (Control + x followed by b), allowing you to keep various projects open and accessible without cluttering your mental space. As you become more accustomed to switching between buffers, you will develop a reflex similar to that of an archer switching between targets with fluidity and purpose.

Navigating through buffers can effectively enhance your productivity, especially when you become adept at leveraging commands like C-x g to list all open buffers. This command functions like a archer's sight, helping you quickly locate your target without hesitation. If you wish to clean up your workspace, C-x k allows you to kill (close) a buffer, ensuring that your focus remains clear and undistracted.

Next, let's examine the minibuffer, a crucial aspect of your interface that runs at the bottom of the Emacs window. The minibuffer is where you enter commands, interact with prompts, and manage file operations. Engaging with the minibuffer is akin to taking a deep, measured breath before releasing an arrow—it requires focus and clarity. When you call a command with M-x (Alt + x), you activate the minibuffer, where you can type the name of any function or command. The minibuffer not only helps you issue commands but also provides feedback on the execution of your tasks, instilling a sense of awareness for every action taken within your coding environment.

Being proficient with the minibuffer will deepen your coding practice by promoting efficiency. For instance, when you want to open a file, simply invoke the command C-x C-f to initiate the process, using the minibuffer to navigate through directories. Mastering this interaction significantly reduces friction in your workflow, allowing you to maintain your flow state much like an archer who moves smoothly between preparation and execution.

The menu bar is another important feature, positioned at the very top of the Emacs window. You can explore the menus for access to various functions, options, and commands. Occasionally, relying on the menu bar can provide visual guidance, similar to a visual aid during archery practice. While relying on keyboard commands enhances speed, the menu bar serves as a helpful reference for new or complex commands that you may not have committed to memory yet.

Modes in Emacs provide tailored experiences depending on the kind of work you are doing—like the variation in techniques an archer will use depending on the type of bow or arrow. Major modes define the syntax highlighting, indentation, and commands available for different file types, such as programming languages or markup languages. Minor modes augment your workflow with additional functionalities, such as autocompletion or text formatting.

Understanding how to switch modes effectively is critical for maximizing your productivity. You can switch major modes using the M-x command followed by the appropriate mode name, while minor modes can often be enabled or disabled simply with keybindings or commands relevant to the functionality they provide. By recognizing the needs of your current project and adjusting your modes accordingly, you become an adept coder able to adapt to any conditions, thus increasing your precision in navigating the complexities of your programming tasks.

As you interact with the interface, keep in mind the importance of customizing your experience. Emacs is an inherently flexible tool, allowing you to configure the layout and functions to reflect your unique coding style, which can be seen as an expression of your identity as a Zen archer. Personalizing your interface—whether through adjustments in keybindings, configuring toolbars, or modifying your themes—ensures that your workspace resonates with you and fosters clarity. Incorporate features that help you work efficiently without strain, ensuring your coding sessions are productive and engaging.

Keyboard commands are the linchpin of effective navigation in Emacs, and fluency in them transforms your workflow, much as an archer's muscle memory aids in rapid and accurate shooting. In the spirit of the Zen archer, practice your commands with intent, reflecting on the fluidity of your movements. For instance, embrace the use of the C-g command to easily quit any ongoing operation or cancel inputs in the minibuffer, allowing you to release any frustration or hindrance and reposition yourself for focus.

Furthermore, take time to learn and explore additional commands and non-linear workflows through the community and available resources like documentation and tutorials. Engage in the ongoing conversation among Emacs users, drawing inspiration and techniques from collective knowledge. Like a community of archers on a range sharing tips and refining skills, this exchange can significantly elevate your interactions with Emacs.

In summary, as you learn to navigate the Emacs interface, approach each element with an open mind and a focus on harmony and function. Allow the components to work together symbiotically as you refine your coding practice to hit your targets with precision. This mindful navigation will create a seamless workflow, elevating your coding experience to align with the Zen archery metaphor—a balanced blend of focus, intuition, and mastery in every keystroke. Breathe, focus, and shoot straight; with each interaction in Emacs, embrace the journey of coding as both an art and a science.

2.4. Extending Emacs Functionality

To extend Emacs functionality is akin to equipping a Zen archer with a variety of arrows tuned to different targets and situations. Just as a master archer carefully selects their tools to maximize performance, so too must a coder enrich their Emacs environment to create a coding powerhouse tailored to their needs. This journey into extensibility is about not merely enhancing productivity but embarking on a personal exploration of possibilities that align with your coding philosophy.

The power of Emacs lies within its highly extensible architecture, primarily powered by a domain-specific programming language known as Emacs Lisp. This capability allows users to add custom features, improve workflows, and integrate tools that facilitate various aspects of coding. When you extend Emacs, you are not just adding functionalities; you are precisely sculpting your environment to resonate with your vision as a coder.

First, consider the rich repository of packages available through the Emacs package manager, a system designed to facilitate the effortless integration of additional features and utilities. Just like selecting arrows from a quiver, you can choose the right packages that resonate with the challenges and tasks you tackle regularly. To begin, accessing the package manager is straightforward: invoke the `M-x package-list-packages` command to explore available options. This command is the doorway to a plethora of resources where each package can be seen as a potential weapon in your coding arsenal, prepped and ready for deployment.

Begin with fundamental packages that significantly enhance your coding experience. The `company-mode`, for instance, offers an auto-completion framework that learns and adapts to your coding patterns, serving as an excellent assistant in writing code efficiently. Efficient suggestions delivered incessantly, or as needed, help maintain your focus, akin to the way an archer plans each shot with the right guidance.

Another powerful addition to your arsenal is `projectile`, which enhances project management capabilities in Emacs. This package allows you to easily navigate directories, switch files, and conduct searches across your projects, streamlining your workflow. Using `projectile`, you can manage multiple projects with the ease of an archer shifting focus between arrows, ensuring you maintain an organized workspace conducive to creative coding.

As you deepen your coding interactions, consider integrating `magit`, an exceptional Git interface. This integration offers version control functionalities seamlessly within Emacs, reducing the friction of context-switching between your code and version control commands. It empowers you to view diffs, commit changes, and manage branches intuitively—all critical aspects of development. This reflects the Zen practice of remaining centered and aware, maintaining momentum during the coding process.

If your work involves extensive documentation or notes, the acclaimed `org-mode` will become an invaluable ally. This package transcends traditional note-taking, allowing you to organize thoughts, projects, and coding tasks efficiently. `Org-mode` helps you create structured documents, track progress, and revisit processes with clarity, much like an archer analyzing their technique after every round. Each entry can serve as a reminder, a goal, or an idea, fostering a mindful approach to your coding journey.

While core packages enhance functionality, don't overlook the opportunity to create your own custom workflows through personal functions written in Emacs Lisp. This step may seem intimidating, but you can begin with small modifications or tweaks to existing functions. Each change can create a seamless flow in your coding rhythm, transforming repetitive tasks into one-command actions, allowing you to code with precision and purpose.

To complement your customizations, keybindings play a crucial role in your workflow. The true power of Emacs lies in its ability to be personalized on an intimate level, much like adjusting the draw weight on a bow. By configuring keybindings effectively, you can craft a suite of shortcuts tailored to fit your coding style. This nimbleness allows for quicker navigation and enhanced productivity, creating a responsive environment where you can effortlessly shift between tasks.

Furthermore, extending your setup shouldn't only focus on adding functionalities but must also account for your own comfort. Create a comfortable workspace that minimizes distractions. Packages like `ace-window` allow for easy navigation between open windows through simple, memorable keybindings. The ease of switching windows can preserve your focus, ensuring you remain immersed in coding like an archer remaining calm amidst external disturbances.

Complex coding tasks require tools that facilitate better debugging and error-handling within your workflow. Here, integrating packages like `flycheck` can elevate your coding experience by providing on-the-fly syntax checking. It allows you to instantly identify potential issues as you code, maintaining accuracy akin to an archer who adjusts their aim with immediate feedback.

Finally, consider the global Emacs community, which embodies collaboration and the pursuit of knowledge shared across boundaries. Engaging with forums, mailing lists, or community-contributed showcase projects can inspire you. The collective wisdom of experienced Emacs users can help guide you in discovering new packages or techniques that resonate with your coding practice. Participation in the community allows your skills to flourish—just as an archer enhances their accuracy through shared insights from peers.

In conclusion, extending the functionality of Emacs is an intentional act of weaving together custom tools and features into a singular, harmonious workflow. The journey is deeply personal and transformative—enabling you to harness Emacs's full potential to create a coding experience that feels as natural and instinctive as the release of an arrow. Embrace the possibilities with an open mind, and select the right tools that align with your individual practice, allowing for a flourishing and mindful coding journey ahead. Through each extension and skillful integration, you'll find yourself hitting the bullseye with every coding shot.

2.5. Customizing Emacs Keybindings

Keybindings in Emacs are quintessential to enhancing your coding experience, acting like instinctive movements ingrained through practice akin to the motions of a Zen archer drawing their bow. Keybindings allow you to navigate swiftly, execute commands efficiently, and mold Emacs into an environment that responds intuitively to your coding reflexes. Customizing keybindings transforms routine operations into fluid actions, making your workflow smoother and more efficient, which is essential to maintaining focus and elevating your productivity.

To begin your journey into customizing Emacs keybindings, it's vital to understand Emacs's fundamental framework for key bindings. Emacs employs a sequence of modifier keys, each equipped with unique functions. These include Control (C), Meta (M - typically the Alt key), and Super (s), each serving as modifiers that combine with other keys to form commands. Crafting personalized keybindings leverages this flexibility, allowing you to designate combinations that resonate with your workflow and memory.

Start by identifying common commands or operations that you perform regularly. These may include opening files, switching buffers, formatting code, or initiating searches. Like an archer carefully selecting frequently used arrows for easy access, you should pinpoint key actions that would benefit from a more convenient keybinding.

For instance, if you often find yourself toggling between two specific files, you can create a custom binding for this operation. Use the following example to illustrate how to define your custom keybinding in your `init.el` configuration file. Here is a simplistic implementation:

```
(global-set-key (kbd "C-c o") 'your-custom-function)
```

In this example, the `C-c o` key combination is linked to `your-custom-function`, an arbitrary function you define. This allows you to trigger it instantly, creating a seamless experience while coding.

Furthermore, consider your coding style and preferences. If you're a programmer who frequently engages in file navigation, you may wish to combine two operations—parsing a buffer and jumping to a definition. By implementing a custom keybinding that combines these commands into a single keystroke sequence, you streamline your workflow significantly. One practical method is using the `kbd` function to create meaningful shortcuts:

```
(global-set-key (kbd "C-c j") 'jump-to-definition-function)
(global-set-key (kbd "C-c p") 'parse-buffer-function)
```

Beyond just creating custom keybindings, the process of grouping functions under specific modifiers will enhance your reflexive interactions with the Emacs environment. Grouping commands sharing a thematic connection can help you remember key sequences better. For example, you could bind all project-related commands to a single prefix key, thus simplifying access:

```
(define-prefix-command 'project-prefix)
(global-set-key (kbd "C-c p") 'project-prefix)
(global-set-key (kbd "C-c p b") 'project-build-function)
(global-set-key (kbd "C-c p r") 'project-run-function)
```

Now, pressing `C-c p` gives you access to project management commands without cluttering your keybindings, much like an archer focusing on a series of shots with a unified goal. This organization can help reduce cognitive load, allowing you to concentrate solely on your coding tasks.

Moreover, Emacs offers numerous packages that inherently enrich keybinding options. Exploring these packages can uncover additional functionality that complements your personalized setup. A prominent example is `evil-mode`, which introduces vim-like modal editing into Emacs. By adopting modal keybindings, you can hone your efficiency, much as a proficient archer benefits from adjusting their stance based on the shooting range.

To delve deeper into customizing keybindings, consider exploring the `which-key` package. This invaluable tool serves as an on-demand keybinding reference, presenting convenient visual hints for available shortcuts. With `which-key`, you reduce the reliance on memorization alone, allowing your focus to remain on the task rather than recalling the myriad of key sequences. It serves to remind you of available commands in a subtle, non-intrusive manner—similar to an archer glance before selecting an arrow from their quiver.

When reflecting on your keybindings, be mindful of avoiding overlap with existing or common Emacs commands to prevent confusion. The conflict can lead to mistakes during critical coding situations. Regularly auditing your keybindings to identify any issues or inefficiencies is akin to an archer consistently practicing to refine their aim and technique.

Additionally, it is essential to recognize the importance of documentation and resources. The Emacs community thrives on shared knowledge and collaboration; thus, exploring forums, GitHub repositories, or even videos showcases best practices and techniques will deepen your understanding of customizing keybindings effectively.

As you become more attuned to your keybinding setup, you may also explore conditional bindings based on the context of your coding environment. Emacs allows this through mode-specific keybindings, meaning you can have one set of key commands active in a programming mode (such as Python or JavaScript) and another set in a text-mode. This adaptability is akin to an archer who adjusts their approach based on the type of target or distance from the target. Context-aware keybindings ensure maximum efficiency while allowing you to stay focused on adaptively responding to your coding needs.

Finally, embrace the iterative journey of refining and optimizing your keybindings over time. As you evolve in your coding practice, so too should your binding configurations adapt to your changing workflow, newfound skills, and specific project requirements. Each iteration allows you to hone your system to better serve your needs, creating a workspace that breathes with your personal coding rhythm.

In conclusion, customizing Emacs keybindings represents a fundamental aspect of optimizing your coding practice. Through mindful selection, organization, and reflection, you can create an intuitive and efficient coding environment that flows with the grace of a Zen archer. Let every keystroke be deliberate and purposeful, capturing the essence of Zen mindfulness that enhances both your coding journey and personal mastery in the craft. As you embark on this path, remember that each configuration is an opportunity—an arrow drawn back, ready to be released toward your coding bullseye.

3. The Zen Art of Focus

3.1. The Breath of Code

The act of coding is deeply intertwined with mindful presence, and it can be tremendously enhanced when approached with the same awareness as a Zen practitioner. In Zen practices, the breath serves as a focal point, a tool to cultivate awareness and promote tranquility. Likewise, in the world of coding, anchoring ourselves to our breath allows for a centered state of mind that can significantly influence our productivity and creativity. Thus, understanding "The Breath of Code" encompasses methods to enhance focus and mindfulness, turning coding from a mechanical task into an artistic pursuit resonating with clarity and intention.

Rooted in the art of coding, the concept of breath can be likened to the rhythm and flow of keystrokes, each line of code representing a moment—an expression of thought captured in written form. Breathing techniques can not only help in grounding ourselves during intensive coding sessions but also serve as a form of meditation, allowing us to detach from stress and distractions. This practice encourages a mindful state where thoughts can be organized and creativity can flourish.

To begin, let's explore the practice of rhythmic breathing—a technique that can be effortlessly integrated into coding sessions. This technique involves inhaling and exhaling in a paced manner, usually at a count of four. For instance, inhale deeply through the nose, allowing the diaphragm to expand for a count of four, hold for a moment to absorb that energy, then exhale slowly for another count of four. This simple cycle can be repeated a handful of times at the beginning of a coding session, establishing a calm and focused atmosphere that primes your mind for work.

Incorporating breath breaks at regular intervals is another effective practice. Similar to an archer who steadies their breath before taking a shot, programmers can pause every 25 to 30 minutes to perform a brief breathing exercise. During these intervals, step away from your screen, close your eyes, and practice a few minutes of deep breathing; this encourages relaxation and reduces the build-up of tension that can occur during prolonged periods of focus. By allowing the mind to reset, you can return to your work with renewed clarity and energy, ready to tackle challenges with sharpened focus.

The breath can also be a tool for centering thoughts when faced with hurdles or cognitive blocks while coding. When you encounter an error in your code or grapple with a complex problem, resorting to your breath can guide you back to a space of calmness and problem-solving clarity. Take a moment to acknowledge any frustration, then engage in a series of deep breaths, visualizing each inhale as an influx of insight and each exhale releasing tension and confusion. This method not only helps in regaining focus but reinforces your resolve, turning obstacles into opportunities for creativity and innovation.

As you navigate through code, consider the relationship between breath and pacing. The cadence of your coding can mirror your breathing patterns; deliberate, mindful pauses align with slower, deeper breaths, allowing for thoughtful reflections on the code being written. Rather than rushing through sections of code, pause at the end of significant blocks and take a breath. This practice encourages a deeper engagement with your work, allowing for clarity in understanding and execution. It's about crafting a relationship with your code that feels intentional—one where each section resonates thoughtfully before you progress onward.

Moreover, fostering an understanding of the space around you as an extension of your breathing can enhance your coding experience. A cluttered environment can evoke stress and distraction, making it difficult to focus. Just as clear breathing allows for a clear mind, a tidy workspace can facilitate productivity. Prioritize organizing your coding space—both physical and digital. Decluttering your working environment sets the stage for enhanced clarity, encouraging a smoother flow akin to the unimpeded rhythm of breathing.

In the spirit of Zen practice, nurturing the breath serves as a reminder to maintain a balance between effort and ease in your coding journey. It encourages a dynamic interplay between focus and relaxation, steering clear of burnout or overwhelming stress. With every coding project, embrace the idea of breath as a catalyst for transformation —allow it to ground you at each step, focusing your thoughts and guiding your actions.

Ultimately, understanding "The Breath of Code" elevates coding from mere technical execution to a mindful practice of creation. By adopting breathing techniques and integrating mindful presence, each coding session becomes an opportunity to cultivate awareness, enrich creativity, and produce code that reflects clarity and purpose. With each keystroke, you breathe life into ideas, crafting solutions with the confidence and focus reminiscent of a Zen archer aiming for the bullseye. Embrace the union of breath and coding, and you open pathways to deeper engagement, enhanced focus, and a profound sense of fulfillment in your work.

3.2. Managing Mindful Work Sessions

Managing mindful work sessions is about creating a structured yet flexible framework for coding that maximizes focus and productivity, while also ensuring that you avoid burnout and maintain a clear mind. Just as a Zen archer employs a disciplined practice to hone their skills, so too must a coder balance their coding sessions with mindfulness and intentional breaks. By adopting techniques that center on dividing work into focused intervals, you can achieve a state of heightened awareness and enhanced productivity.

Begin by implementing the technique of time management known as the Pomodoro Technique. This method, named after the Italian word for tomato (referencing the timers used in this approach), is founded on the principle of working in intense bursts followed by short breaks. The classic structure involves working for 25 minutes and then taking a 5-minute break, with longer breaks after every four sessions. This pattern allows for sustained concentration during the work period and provides intervals where the mind can rest. The key is to fully immerse yourself during the work block while allowing your mind the luxury of rest during the breaks, thereby preventing mental fatigue.

When employing the Pomodoro Technique, consider the nature of your work sessions. For focused coding, ensure that you select specific tasks that can be accomplished within the time frame. A well-defined task will draw you into a flow state, where challenges are met with creativity rather than overwhelming stress. Write down your tasks beforehand to create a roadmap for your session. This preparation mirrors an archer's pre-competition warm-up, allowing you to visualize your goals before you take aim.

During each work session, cultivate an awareness of your breathing—an essential tool for fostering mindfulness amidst the variable pace of coding tasks. As you begin a focused block of work, consciously take a few deep breaths to settle your thoughts. With every inhale, bring your attention to the activity at hand, reinforcing your intention to stay present. Every exhale can symbolize releasing distractions and external pressures. This practice roots you firmly in the moment, which is invaluable as coding can often stimulate a flood of intersecting thoughts and ideas.

Embrace the idea of intentional distractions during your breaks. When the timer signals the end of your work session, instead of mindlessly scrolling through social media or checking emails, choose activities that foster rejuvenation and reflection. Step away from your workstation, stretch your limbs, hydrate, or engage in a brief mindful meditation. Such activities invigorate your mind, aligning with the principles of Zen, which emphasize the necessity of balance between effort and repose.

Additionally, consider the importance of a comfortable workspace when planning your work sessions. An organized and aesthetically pleasing environment enhances your focus and reduces potential distractions. Just as an archer prepares their physical space for optimal shooting, ensure that your coding environment is conducive to focused work. Eliminate clutter, set a comfortable temperature, and pay attention to lighting, as all these factors can influence your mental state. Use soft, ambient lighting to create a calm atmosphere, and strive for an ergonomic workspace that encourages proper posture to avoid fatigue.

Variables can, however, disrupt waves of focus during coding sessions. Acknowledge this reality and anticipate potential distractions. Prepare tools and strategies for handling interruptions, such as employing a "Do Not Disturb" sign, silencing notifications on your devices, or informing colleagues of your focused periods. This proactive approach empowers you to reclaim your time during each work block, similar to how an archer mentally blocks distractions while focusing on their target.

As you guide yourself through coding tasks, reflect on the art of pacing. Just as an archer must time their shots and manage their mental energy over a competition, you too should manage the intensity of your work during different stages. Acknowledge that not every session will yield the same level of output and following intense sessions, consider integrating lighter days focused on learning or code reviewing, allowing you to balance output without succumbing to burnout.

Lastly, build in moments for reflection at the conclusion of each coding session. Take time at the end of your work cycle to journal your accomplishments, challenging moments, and lessons learned during your focused work. This not only aids in reinforcing your growth mindset but also allows you to celebrate small victories—all of which contribute to a fulfilling coding journey.

In summary, managing mindful work sessions acts as a canvas upon which you can paint your coding practice with intent, purpose, and clarity. By segmenting work into focused intervals, acknowledging the importance of breaks, cultivating a conducive environment, and practicing intentional reflection, you elevate your coding experience to that of a Zen archer. Each shot is a blend of targeted focus and mindful execution, guiding you steadily towards your coding aspirations whilst nurturing your well-being along the way.

3.3. Creating a Zen-Inducing Environment

Creating a workspace that promotes calmness and focus is essential for achieving optimal coding efficiency. When approaching the design of your coding environment, it's vital to consider both the psychological and physical aspects that can drastically impact your productivity. A Zen-inducing environment encourages mindfulness, minimizes distractions, and fosters creativity—elements that are critical for any coder dedicated to achieving mastery.

Start with the foundational layout of your workspace. A well-structured arrangement should prioritize comfort and functionality while reflecting clarity and simplicity. Position your computer screen at eye level to reduce neck strain and maintain proper posture—an ergonomic setup is akin to an archer adjusting their stance for accuracy. Your desk should be free from clutter, as unnecessary items can become distractions that draw your focus away from the task at hand. This minimalistic approach embodies the spirit of Zen, with each item serving a purpose and contributing to a peaceful ambiance.

In terms of aesthetics, the colors and materials used in your workspace matter significantly. Subtle tones such as soft greens, grays, and blues are known to evoke tranquility and calmness—qualities that can enhance your coding sessions. Incorporating natural elements, such as plants or wooden decorations, can further promote a sense of peace. These elements can act as reminders of nature, grounding you amidst the digital realm and connecting you to a broader environment, much like how an archer finds balance through their connection to the bow and arrow.

Lighting plays a critical role in creating a conducive workspace. Favor natural light sources whenever possible, as they improve mood and reduce eye strain. Position your desk in proximity to windows or opt for daylight bulbs that replicate the effects of sunlight. In the evening or during low-light conditions, utilize task lighting with adjustable brightness to maintain comfort. The gentle glow of well-placed lamps can create a cozy, inviting atmosphere, allowing you to code for extended periods without fatigue.

Sound is another essential factor to consider. A bustling environment can disrupt focus and lead to inefficiencies. To combat this, find a balance by incorporating calming background sounds, such as soft instrumental music or nature sounds. Alternatively, noise-canceling headphones can help create a personal bubble away from distractions, allowing you to immerse yourself fully in your coding sessions like an archer refining their focus amidst the noise of a competition.

In addition to these sensory elements, the integration of technology can significantly enhance your Zen coding experience. Ensure that your Emacs environment is tailored to suit your coding style, as a customized setup supports your unique workflow. Use themes that are easy on the eyes, like soft color schemes or classic dark backgrounds that reduce glare. Complement this with appropriate font choices—monospaced fonts that are clear and legible will aid in reducing strain while enhancing the clarity of your code.

Make sure to implement organizational systems within your coding environment. Use folders and file structures efficiently, applying naming conventions that resonate with you. Just as an archer organizes their tools for quick access, maintaining a logical system for your projects and files will promote ease of navigation and a clutter-free environment, further enhancing focus.

While physical space is critical, the mental environment you foster while coding also deserves attention. Establish specific coding rituals that signal the start of your work sessions. It could be a short mindfulness meditation or deep breathing exercise that helps you transition into a focus state, preparing your mind for the coding journey ahead. Each session can begin with a few moments of reflection, setting an intention for what you wish to achieve, much like an archer visualizing their aim before releasing an arrow.

Another important aspect is the use of breaks. Incorporating schedule intervals for movement, stretch, or distant focus can help avoid burnout during long sessions. Taking mindful breaks allows you to regroup your thoughts, prevent fatigue, and rejuvenate your energy. During these pauses, engage in activities that allow your mind to wander, or shift your focus away from screens. The act of disengaging from coding can often lead to insights as you allow your subconscious to process information.

Lastly, it's vital to create a sense of community within your workspace, even if you're working remotely. Engaging with peers through virtual coworking sessions or coding meetups can foster camaraderie and accountability, akin to how archers often train together for motivation. Participating in collaborative environments encourages shared knowledge, offers support, and can even mitigate feelings of isolation.

In conclusion, crafting a Zen-inducing environment involves thoughtful attention to the layout, aesthetics, lighting, sound, and organization of your workspace, complemented by intentional mental practices. By aligning your physical setup with a serene mindset, you create an atmosphere that promotes calmness and focus, which are essential for achieving mastery in your coding journey. Each element contributes to a holistic coding experience, allowing you to connect deeply with your craft, much like a Zen archer drawing back their bow, ready to release their thoughts into lines of code with precision and purpose.

3.4. Cultivating Discipline in Code

The path to cultivating discipline in coding is much like the journey of a Zen archer—a quest that requires commitment, reflection, and the forming of habits that enhance skill. Discipline is not merely the implementation of routines; it is a state of mind, a relentless pursuit of improvement and awareness that permeates your coding practices. This section guides you through essential habits and practices that will fortify your coding discipline, allowing you to strike true with every keystroke.

First and foremost, it is essential to establish a consistent coding schedule. Just as an archer dedicates time to practice—whether early in the morning or late in the evening—developing a fixed routine helps cultivate discipline. Set aside specific blocks of time daily or weekly devoted solely to coding. This commitment will create a habitual flow to your work, allowing your mind to anticipate these moments as opportunities for creativity and focus. Consistency builds a rhythm akin to the steady pattern of breathing before taking a bow shot, where anticipation and practice coalesce into excellence.

Alongside defining a schedule, creating a conducive workspace deepens your dedication to discipline. Similar to how an archer finds their most effective shooting stance and surroundings, your coding environment must be tailored to reduce distractions and enhance concentration. Ensure your workspace is organized, removing any clutter that might cloud your focus. Minimize digital distractions by silencing notifications and closing unrelated applications or browser tabs. This intentional approach allows you to immerse yourself entirely in your coding tasks, reinforcing a dedicated mindset that values the process.

Reflection is another key habit in cultivating discipline. After each coding session, take time to assess your progress, understanding what worked and what did not. This practice mirrors an archer's assessment after training—reviewing sights, techniques, and focus points for improvement. Consider keeping a coding journal where you document insights, roadblocks, and solutions. This written reflection will not only sharpen your awareness of your coding journey but also set the stage for future growth, reinforcing a continuous improvement mindset.

Moreover, embrace a growth mindset characterized by curiosity and openness to learning. Recognize that discipline involves understanding the limits of your current capabilities and exploring ways to expand them. Set specific, achievable goals for each coding session, ranging from learning a new function to completing a project milestone. This process serves dual purposes: it provides direction in your work while challenging you to step outside your comfort zone. As an archer must continually improve their aim, so too must a coder strive for greater understanding and mastery of their craft.

Integration of mindfulness techniques further empowers your discipline. Mindfulness in coding entails bringing intentional focus to each task at hand, resisting the urge to rush through code or get lost in the myriad of distractions. Periodically pause during your session—close your eyes, take a deep breath, and bring awareness to your thoughts. This moment of reflection cultivates a sense of presence, enhancing your connection with the code you write and allowing insights to arise more organically. Much like an archer who pauses to visualize their shot before release, lending space to thought fosters profound concentration.

Another facet of cultivating discipline is the practice of feedback and collaboration. Seek opportunities to engage with peers or mentors, allowing the exchange of ideas and constructive feedback to enrich your coding practice. Group coding sessions can simulate a supportive training environment akin to archery clubs or practices, where members encourage one another to push boundaries and refine techniques. Participate in code reviews, both giving and receiving critiques, to foster continuous improvement through shared experiences.

As your coding discipline grows, remember to embrace challenges as learning opportunities. Coding is inherently fraught with puzzles, bugs, and moments of frustration—each one presenting a chance to refine your approach and reinforce your resolve. Just as an archer recalibrates after a miss, reflect on your challenges and view them as stepping stones toward growth. This perspective allows you to remain motivated when faced with difficulty, turning obstacles into catalysts for progress.

In parallel, leverage resources available to you—be they online courses, coding boot camps, tutorials, or forums—to further enhance your skill development. The tech community is vast, offering myriad opportunities for learning and growth. Engaging with external resources encourages a more disciplined approach to ongoing education, mirroring an archer's commitment to honing their abilities through diverse training methods.

Finally, allow yourself space for rest and recovery. True discipline does not equate to relentless hustle; instead, it acknowledges the importance of balance. Taking breaks, reflecting on your work, and allowing yourself time to recharge are vital to maintaining a sustainable practice. Integrate periods of reflection where you detach from the code and assess your mental well-being; these moments keep you grounded and focused on the larger journey ahead.

In closing, cultivating discipline in coding is an ongoing process of commitment, reflection, and learning. Embrace each day as an opportunity to sharpen your skills, create a dedicated workspace, and promote a growth mindset that values progress. As you embark on this path, remember the words of the Zen master: discipline is not about the end goal; it is the art of unfolding your potential through consistent, mindful practice. As you cultivate your discipline in code, you will discover the profound connection between mastery and a mindful approach—one that allows you to hit the coding bullseye with clarity and precision every time.

3.5. The Balance of Form and Function

The intersection of form and function is a delicate balance that lies at the core of effective coding practices. This idea is not only critical in understanding how to write code that accomplishes its intended tasks efficiently but also how to present that code in a manner that is clean, understandable, and aesthetically pleasing. Much like an archer's stance and the grace with which they draw and release their bow, a coder must approach their craft with an awareness of both the logical flow of their code and the visual structure that surrounds it.

Form refers to the syntax and structure of the code—the rules and conventions that govern how programming languages are written. Function, on the other hand, deals with the logical components and algorithms that give the code its purpose and meaning. Striking the right balance ensures that code is not only operational but also maintainable over time. In this context, we delve into the practices that promote an equilibrium between form and function, enhancing the clarity, efficiency, and elegance of your code.

To begin with, understanding the importance of readability in your code is paramount. Just as an archer must accurately align their shot through sight and focus, a coder must ensure that their code is legible to other developers. Clear naming conventions for functions, variables, and classes play a critical role in achieving this. Opt for descriptive names that convey their purpose without being excessively verbose or cryptic. This practice reflects both form and function—creating an architecture that is intuitive while serving its logical needs.

Comments and documentation further support this balance. They provide context to the form of the code, enhancing comprehension when revisiting the codebase or collaborating with others. Thoughtful comments can clarify complex sections of code, akin to the guidance a mentor provides to a novice archer, helping them refine their technique. However, it's essential to adopt a disciplined approach to commenting; excessive or redundant commentary can lead to clutter, obscuring the intended meaning much like an overcrowded shooting range creates chaos amid tranquility.

In programming, adhering to coding standards and style guides also contributes to the aesthetics of the codebase. Whether you follow established guidelines like PEP 8 for Python or the Google Java Style Guide, consistency in indentation, spacing, and overall structure allows the code to flow as seamlessly as an archer's draw. Establishing a standard among team members cultivates a shared understanding, minimizing cognitive overload and fostering collaboration.

Beyond readability, performance optimization ties back into function. An elegant solution is not only one that is easy to read but also efficient in execution. This involves recognizing performance bottlenecks and addressing them through thoughtful algorithms and data structures. Employing design patterns effectively is akin to an archer choosing the appropriate technique for each shot; understanding the strengths and trade-offs of various approaches leads to more informed decisions in coding.

Refactoring emerges as a pivotal practice in maintaining the dual integrity of form and function. As projects evolve, so must the code itself. Regularly revisiting and refining sections of your code enhances clarity and performance. This practice mirrors an archer who revisits their technique following each practice session—ensuring that their form remains precise and aligned with their intended outcomes. Refactoring avoids technical debt, where poorly structured code accumulates over time, making future modifications cumbersome and prone to errors.

Moreover, unit testing serves as an essential procedure to uphold this balance. By writing tests to verify that your code functions as intended, you ensure that changes made during refactoring do not introduce new bugs. The validation process enforces a disciplined approach to coding, emphasizing not only functionality but also the need for reliable performance—much like an archer ensuring their equipment is in optimal condition before a competition.

In the realm of code reviews, discussions around form and function become vital. Engaging with peers to critique and improve each other's work bridges the gap between aesthetics and logic. Peer feedback offers diverse perspectives, often unveiling insights that one may overlook in isolation. This collective refinement process yields code that is not only sound in logic but also resonates with elegance and organization.

Finally, as the digital landscape continues to evolve, the adaptability to integrate new technologies without compromising existing codebases is crucial. Just as an archer must adjust their technique to suit different conditions or targets, a coder must be attentive to emerging languages, frameworks, and tools that can enhance both form and function. Staying updated on best practices and new paradigms amplifies one's ability to write code that fulfills contemporary and future needs.

In conclusion, the balance between form and function in coding is an art that requires ongoing practice and mindfulness. By placing emphasis on readability, performance, consistency, and continuous improvement, developers can rise to the level of Zen archers—attuning their craft to hit the bullseye of coding excellence with each keystroke. The journey toward mastering this balance is not merely a technical endeavor; it is a holistic one that fosters integrity in code and illuminates the beauty of well-crafted programming solutions. As we move forward in our coding paths, let us remain vigilant stewards of this balance, creating work that resonates with both clarity and purpose.

4. Archery Techniques Applied to Coding

4.1. The Zen Archer's Posture

The posture of a Zen archer, much like the approach to coding, is paramount for achieving excellence and maintaining longevity in your practice. In this exploration, we will delve into the crucial elements of physical ergonomics that not only enhance your comfort during long coding sessions but also resonate with the Zen principles of focus, awareness, and intentionality.

An essential aspect of effective posture is understanding the setup of your workstation. Just as an archer meticulously arranges their equipment for optimal performance, your coding environment must support your body to minimize fatigue and maximize focus. Start by establishing an ergonomic setup: your chair should provide adequate lumbar support, allowing your back to maintain its natural curve. Not only does this prevent discomfort during prolonged periods of coding, but it also ensures that your mind remains alert and engaged.

Your desk height plays a critical role in achieving a balanced posture. Ideally, your elbows should be at a 90-degree angle, relaxed at your sides while your hands float comfortably over the keyboard. This configuration mirrors the stable stance of an archer, allowing for controlled, precise movements that prevent strain. If possible, consider using a height-adjustable desk, which allows you to alternate between sitting and standing positions, promoting blood flow and alleviating the tension built up during long coding stretches.

In addition to chair and desk height, the alignment of your screen is vital. Position your monitor at eye level so that your neck remains relaxed and your gaze is slightly downward. An upper-body tilt can lead to neck and shoulder strain over time, disrupting your concentration much like improper form would impact an archer's shot trajectory. By aligning your screen to your natural line of sight, you reduce discomfort and keep your focus firmly on the code at hand.

Taking time to establish healthy wrist positioning is equally essential. As you type, ensure that your wrists maintain a neutral position, neither bent up or down. Utilize a wrist rest if necessary, which serves as a cushion to elevate your wrists, avoiding undue pressure during prolonged periods of typing. This sensitivity to body mechanics echoes the meticulous nature of an archer, who understands that every minor adjustment affects the efficacy of their shot.

Yet just as the archer must also tune their mental state, so too must the coder be conscious of their mental posture. This involves cultivating a mindset that is open, present, and resilient, allowing for creative problem-solving when faced with challenges. Engage in mindful breathing exercises throughout your coding sessions, pausing periodically to take deep, intentional breaths to center yourself. Inhale deeply, expanding your diaphragm and filling your lungs; hold for a moment, and then exhale fully. This practice not only fosters relaxation but can also renew your focus, imbuing each keystroke with clarity and purpose.

Moreover, frequent breaks are vital in maintaining both physical and mental wellness. The concept of the Pomodoro Technique—working for focused intervals followed by short breaks—mirrors the practice of an archer who takes time to reset their stance between shots. Use this structure to step away from your screen, stretch your limbs, and allow your body to reset before returning to the rhythm of coding. These regulated breaks can aid circulation, prevent burnout, and rejuvenate your mind.

Mindfulness also extends to your workflow and the way you approach problem-solving within the code. Embrace a simplistic mantra—"slow and steady"—both in your physical movements and in the way you engage with challenging tasks. As you write code, let go of the pressure to rush to completion; instead, cultivate a reflective mindset and appreciate the nuances of the process. This deliberate approach aligns with the principles of Zen, which value the journey over merely reaching the destination.

Ultimately, the zen archer's posture—both physically and mentally —serves as a vital metaphor for coding practice. By nurturing an ergonomic workspace that encourages comfort, fostering a mindset grounded in mindfulness and intent, and maintaining a rhythm of focused effort balanced with restorative breaks, you create a holistic environment conducive to success. Each coding session becomes another opportunity to refine not just your technical skills but also your awareness of self—an integral aspect of mastering your craft.

In summary, by paralleling the physical posture of a Zen archer with the mental awareness required for coding, you cultivate a practice that transcends technical ability. It enriches your coding journey, ensuring that each line of code is infused with intention and grace—leading you ever closer to the bullseye of mindful programming.

4.2. Setting Targets and Goals

Setting clear targets and goals is pivotal in directing your coding practice, providing a roadmap that guides your efforts with precision, much like an archer focusing on the bullseye before every shot. By establishing concrete, well-defined objectives, you create a structured path to progress—one that can help prevent distraction and encourage consistent improvement. This approach not only enhances your productivity but also promotes a deeper engagement with your coding journey.

The first step in setting effective coding targets involves understanding the difference between short-term and long-term goals. Short-term goals are achievable within a matter of days or weeks, offering immediate feedback and motivation. These could include tasks like completing a specific coding challenge, fixing bugs in a project, or learning to use a new library or framework. By breaking down larger objectives into smaller, actionable tasks, you mirror the archery practice of incrementally working on technique, ensuring each session builds upon the last.

Long-term goals, on the other hand, stretch across months or even years and often revolve around broader aspirations, such as mastering a programming language, contributing to an open-source project, or achieving proficiency in a particular technology. Here, visualization plays a critical role: just as an archer envisions their shot before releasing the arrow, you should picture the end result of your long-term goals. Envisioning success fosters motivation, helps you identify necessary steps, and reinforces your commitment to the path ahead.

To effectively set your targets, employ the SMART criteria—making your goals Specific, Measurable, Achievable, Relevant, and Time-bound. For instance, instead of stating a vague goal like "I want to improve my coding skills," reframe it to "I will complete three coding exercises on LeetCode each week for the next month." Such specificity provides clarity and assurance, while the measurable aspect allows you to track your progress and adjust your strategies as necessary.

In addition to setting individual goals, it's beneficial to align them with your broader values and aspirations within the coding realm. Reflect on what drives your passion for coding—be it problem-solving, creativity, or technological innovation. Understanding your intrinsic motivation serves as a foundation that fuels both your short- and long-term goals, ensuring they resonate with your identity as a coder. This reflects the notion of purpose in Zen practice, where actions align with the practitioner's true self, leading to greater fulfillment in the journey.

As you embark on this goal-setting journey, it's vital to maintain flexibility and adaptability. Just as an archer must adjust their stance or technique based on feedback and changing conditions, you too will encounter unforeseen challenges and shifts in priorities. Embrace a mindset that welcomes recalibration of your goals; if a target proves overly ambitious or if new opportunities arise, adjust your course thoughtfully.

Documenting your goals and reviewing them regularly is also essential. Keep a dedicated journal or digital workspace where you can outline your targets, jot down thoughts, and reflect on your progress. This practice mirrors the reflection an archer undergoes after each training session; it cultivates an awareness of your growth and the areas needing attention. Regular review allows you to celebrate achievements, sparking motivation to push further, while also identifying patterns or obstacles that may hinder your progress.

Accountability is another crucial aspect of goal-setting. Engage with peers or mentors who can act as sounding boards—sharing your targets with others not only creates a sense of accountability but may also provide useful support and inspiration. Much like a community of archers who encourage each other and share techniques, collaborating with others can enhance your coding practice and lead to productive exchanges of ideas.

In addition, consider incorporating time for reflection on your goals and progress at the end of each coding session. Taking a moment to analyze what you accomplished against your set targets allows you to stay aware of your trajectory. You may find it beneficial to ask yourself questions such as: What did I achieve today? What challenges did I face? How can I adjust my strategies moving forward?

Revisiting your targets periodically not only refreshes your commitment but can also inspire new visions and aspirations. In doing so, you create an ongoing narrative around your coding journey, one that evolves, reflects, and refines over time.

Lastly, remember to celebrate the milestones you achieve along the way—both big and small. Acknowledging achievements fosters a sense of accomplishment and revitalizes motivation. Whether it's completing a challenging project or reaching a new proficiency level, pausing to appreciate your journey underscores the value of each step taken.

In sum, setting targets and goals is an essential practice that can guide your coding journey with clarity, focus, and intention. By applying principles akin to those of a Zen archer—specificity, adaptability, reflection, and celebration—you equip yourself to navigate the intricacies of coding with purpose. Each goal is a shot aimed toward a larger vision of mastery, ensuring that every keystroke not only moves you closer to the bullseye of your aspirations but also enriches your experience along the way. Embrace the journey with mindfulness, and let your targets propel you forward into the heart of your coding craft.

4.3. The Release: Letting Go of Perfectionism

Perfectionism often manifests as an insidious foe along the coding journey, seducing us into an endless loop of revisions and self-doubt. In coding, as in archery, the pursuit of perfection can lead us astray, shifting focus from aiming for the bullseye to an unattainable standard that hinders our progress. To fully embrace the Zen approach to coding, we must learn to let go of perfectionism, allowing our creative expression to flow freely without the constraints of excessive self-critique.

At its core, perfectionism breeds a fear of failure—one that paralyzes our ability to initiate projects or finalize code. Much like an archer who hesitates to release their arrow due to the fear of imperfection, this hesitation can stifle creativity and productivity. The first step in dismantling this mindset is cultivating an awareness of the thoughts that accompany perfectionism. Examine your internal dialogue: Are you telling yourself that your code must be flawless before showing it to others? Are you waiting until every detail is perfect before you can consider it complete? These narratives can trap you in a cycle of stagnation, preventing you from moving forward.

To counter this, embrace the philosophy of progress over perfection. Shift your focus from achieving an ideal state to celebrating incremental improvements. Just as an archer consistently practices their technique to enhance their skills, engage in short, iterative coding sessions that emphasize continuous progress. This practice can create a feedback loop where each small victory—bug fixes, feature implementations, or simply the completion of a task—reinforces the value of imperfect action. By adopting a mindset of progress, you allow room for experimentation and learning, essential components of any coding journey.

Establishing clear goals can aid in this transition from perfectionism to progress. Define what success looks like for each project phase and set milestones. In doing so, you create opportunities for evaluation and reflection without tying success to unattainable standards. Much like an archer sets a target distance for their practice, you can delineate boundaries for your coding projects, ensuring that they are focused and manageable. Acknowledge that every line of code you write is a step along your journey, contributing to your growth as a developer.

Additionally, consider adopting a philosophy of iteration. Coding practices are rarely linear; instead, they often involve refining ideas and approaches over time. Implement the concept of "release early, release often" to your projects. By deploying early versions, you create pathways for feedback. This collaborative input can alleviate the burden of perfectionism, reminding you that your work is meant to evolve. Similar to an archer who learns from each shot's trajectory, you can harness the insights gained from feedback to continually improve your coding outputs.

Mindfulness practices can further support your journey away from perfectionism. Before initiating a coding session, take a moment to breathe and ground yourself. Allow those moments of stillness to clear the mental clutter that perfectionism creates. In this space of awareness, commit to approaching your work with an open heart and mind, ready to embrace the imperfections that may arise. This connection to the present moment fosters resilience and creativity in your work, acknowledging that imperfections are not failures but stepping stones toward mastery.

Recognizing the intrinsic value of your work is critical in overcoming perfectionism. This practice involves honoring your time, efforts, and ideas, regardless of their imperfections. Reflect on the intention behind your coding endeavors; understand that each line serves a purpose. Just as each arrow shot contributes to the archer's growth, each piece of code has value in shaping your development as a programmer. Allowing yourself to release attachment to outcomes frees you to engage with your craft more authentically.

Finally, embrace the community aspect of coding as an antidote to perfectionism. Engaging with fellow developers—be it through forums, coworking sessions, or study groups—provides opportunities for vulnerability and growth. Sharing your work without the filter of perfection fosters connections and encourages collaboration. Just as archers often train in groups, sharing techniques and experiences, opening yourself to community support can diminish the pressure to strive for unattainable perfection.

In summary, the journey of letting go of perfectionism in coding mirrors the practices of a Zen archer. By focusing on progress, establishing clear goals, embracing iteration, practicing mindfulness, valuing your work, and leaning on community support, you create a harmonious coding practice where creativity flourishes. Allow the release of perfectionism to guide your path as you aim for the coding bullseye, fostering resilience and joy in your practice. Ultimately, it is through this acceptance of imperfection that you will discover the true essence of mastery in your coding journey, propelling your skill and creativity to new heights.

4.4. Adapting to Change: The Archer's Way

Adapting to change is an essential skill for coders, much like a Zen archer who must adjust their aim to account for wind, distance, and target movement. The landscapes of technology and coding are constantly shifting; new programming languages, frameworks, and methodologies emerge rapidly, reshaping the way we solve problems and approach tasks. To thrive in this dynamic environment, one must embrace flexibility and adaptability, skills that are equally vital in both archery and coding.

Understanding the principle of adaptability starts with acknowledging that change is a constant in the coding world. Just as an archer trains in various weather conditions and terrains, coders must be prepared to navigate a wide array of challenges. When faced with a change in technology, be it an upgrade in a programming language, the introduction of a new tool, or a fresh coding paradigm, it is crucial to maintain an open mind and a willingness to learn. This adaptability enables coders to quickly pivot their strategies, allowing them to remain effective and productive.

One of the first steps in adapting to change is cultivating a growth mindset. Embrace mistakes and view them as opportunities for learning and growth. Instead of fearing failure, acknowledge it as an integral part of the journey. Just as an archer learns to adjust their shot after each attempt, programmers must take the time to reflect on coding missteps. Analyzing what went wrong, understanding the underlying reasons, and applying this knowledge to future projects is critical for personal development.

Additionally, staying informed about industry trends and advancements is vital. Engage with the coding community by following blogs, attending meetups, and participating in forums. Much like archers discuss techniques and gear, coders benefit from exchanging knowledge and insights with peers. The collaboration fosters a community of leaners, ensuring you remain current and capable of leveraging new tools and methodologies as they arise.

Furthermore, investing time in self-education can significantly bolster your adaptability. Allocate portions of your coding practice to explore new languages or frameworks outside your comfort zone. Just as an archer hones their skills by trying different bows or shooting techniques, stepping into unfamiliar territory allows you to expand your repertoire. Learning a new language may seem daunting initially, but breaking it down into smaller, manageable tasks can transform the process into an engaging experience.

Flexibility in your coding style also contributes to adaptability. Different projects require varying approaches, ranging from tackling front-end development to diving into back-end programming. A rigid mindset can cause friction during transitions. Instead, cultivate a versatile coding style that enables you to shift between paradigms effortlessly. Challenge yourself to learn about design patterns, coding best practices, or collaborative workflows. This broader knowledge base strengthens your capacity to adapt, just as an archer benefits from understanding different shooting stances for various scenarios.

Moreover, embracing new technologies should not come at the cost of forgetting the fundamentals. Just as a Zen archer must hone their basics consistently, maintain your core skills through regular practice. Ensure you continuously reinforce your understanding of essential coding principles, even while venturing into new domains. This foundational knowledge serves as a bedrock, enhancing your ability to integrate new techniques and tools effectively—ensuring you can adapt without losing sight of your core competencies.

At times, adapting to change may also involve unlearning certain practices that have become ingrained over time. Reflection, self-assessment, and feedback from peers are invaluable in this process. An objective evaluation of your existing approaches can reveal outdated techniques that may hinder progress. Embrace change with grace; unlearning is a skill in and of itself. Acknowledge the inevitable need to let go of practices that no longer serve your goals, allowing yourself to embrace more effective strategies that leverage the capabilities of new technologies.

In a rapidly evolving digital landscape, it is vital to maintain an integrative approach. Consider how changes across disciplines—like shifts toward cloud computing, artificial intelligence, or agile methodologies—may influence your coding practice. Drawing parallels from these changes can inspire new problem-solving techniques and broaden your perspective. An adaptable coder not only responds to existing changes but anticipates future trends, ensuring they remain ahead of the curve.

In conclusion, adapting to change is one of the most essential qualities a coder can develop. By cultivating a growth mindset, staying informed about trends, investing in self-education, exploring new domains, and maintaining a focus on foundational skills, you can secure yourself as a versatile and effective coder in a dynamically changing environment. Like a Zen archer who embraces the wind as part of their shot, you can navigate the turbulence of technological change with confidence and grace, ensuring that you continue to hit the bullseye with each coding endeavor.

4.5. The Follow-through in Coding

The heart of coding lies not just in the lines of code we write, but in the way we carry through our intentions and the clarity we maintain while executing our tasks. Much like an archer who remains focused after releasing an arrow, coders too need to cultivate a robust follow-through in their processes for successful project completion. The follow-through serves as the decisive factor that determines the quality of our coding endeavors, bridging the gap between intention and execution with mindfulness and precision.

Understanding the significance of a strong follow-through in coding begins with recognizing that it encompasses both the final steps of a project and the reflections that occur thereafter. Whether you are writing a new feature, debugging a complex problem, or refactoring existing code, it is crucial to ensure that you bring your efforts to a successful conclusion. This involves not only completing a task but reflecting on the process and results, allowing for continuous growth and development.

To cultivate a meaningful follow-through, start by developing a checklist of final steps that should be undertaken upon completing a coding task. This is akin to the ritual an archer follows after releasing their arrow: a mental and physical checklist that ensures all aspects of the shot have been executed correctly. Your coding checklist might involve reviewing code for readability, running tests to confirm functionality, and ensuring that documentation is updated. Each of these elements contributes to producing a piece of code that is not only functional but also maintainable and comprehensible.

After writing code, dedicate time to perform code reviews. This practice is integral to the follow-through, as it fosters a collaborative spirit and encourages receiving constructive feedback. Just as an archer might study their technique with a coach, engaging in peer reviews helps identify areas for improvement. This process not only contributes to the current project's success but also enhances your skills as a coder over time—turning feedback into actionable insights that you can apply in future coding endeavors.

Another essential component of your follow-through is testing. Incorporate a robust testing framework to validate your work meticulously. Automated tests or unit tests allow you to check if the code behaves as expected and ensures that future changes do not introduce new defects. As an archer would practice regularly to maintain precision in their aim, consistent application of testing reinforces the integrity of your codebase. This cycle of testing and validating fosters confidence, ensuring you understand the outcomes of your efforts before finalizing your contributions.

Moreover, reflections at the completion of tasks encourage a growth mindset. Set aside time after each project or major coding milestone to document what went well and what can be improved. Just as an archer reflects on their last performance to hone their skills, allow your reflections to serve as a formative assessment of your coding decisions, techniques, and mental processes. Write down insights in a coding journal or project retrospective document. This practice highlights both successes and challenges, creating a repository of knowledge you can refer back to in future projects, enriching your skillset along the journey.

Fostering a sustainable codebase additionally requires documentation as part of your follow-through. Ensure that your code is well-documented; this includes comments that clarify complex sections, README files that explain usage, and changelogs that track version history. This kind of documentation is not merely a formality; it serves as a guide for both your future self and others who may interact with your code later on. Much like an archer relies on their equipment specifications to optimize performance, solid documentation empowers all users of your codebase to transition seamlessly into understanding and altering your contributions.

You should also strive to celebrate your achievements along the way. Each coding project finished, each bug resolved, and each feature successfully implemented deserves recognition. This can be an internal celebration—where you acknowledge your effort and growth—or a shared celebration with your team. This reinforces a positive attitude towards productivity, creating a motivating atmosphere and instilling a sense of accomplishment. Celebrating milestones reminds you of the dedication that goes into your craft, much like an archer who savors the satisfaction of making a perfect shot.

The follow-through process is about maintaining a connection to your coding work. It encourages you not to rush through tasks partway but rather to see them through to completion, treating each step with care and attention. Much like an archer finds tranquility in their movements—drawing the bow, aiming, releasing, and reflecting on the shot—coders should strive to engage fully in their practice, ensconced in mindful clarity throughout the entire coding process.

In conclusion, a strong follow-through in coding is a multifaceted practice that integrates review, testing, reflection, and documentation into your workflow. This practice enhances the quality of your code and fosters personal development, turning each endeavor into an opportunity for growth. By embracing this philosophy, you embody the spirit of the Zen archer, ensuring that every coding shot is precise and intentional, ultimately leading to mastery in your craft.

5. Mastering Emacs Skills

5.1. Essential Emacs Commands

Familiarity with essential Emacs commands is pivotal in navigating the Emacs environment effectively. These commands not only enhance productivity but also allow you to channel the fluidity of a Zen archer, deftly moving through your workspace while maintaining focus. Mastering these commands lays a solid foundation for deeper exploration of Emacs's capabilities and supports a mindful coding practice.

To begin with, knowing how to open and save files effectively forms the backbone of your day-to-day interactions in Emacs. You can use C-x C-f to find and open a file, invoking the minibuffer to navigate your filesystem. As you type the path of the file you wish to open, Emacs provides auto-completion options, a feature that embodies the efficiency of disciplined archers who rely on their equipment to streamline their movements. To save changes to the current buffer, execute C-x C-s, ensuring that your hard work is not lost in the depths of code.

Navigating through coupled or multiple buffers is another crucial skill. Each buffer represents a different file or view that you might be working on simultaneously. To switch between these buffers, use C-x b, followed by the name of the buffer you wish to activate. If you need to review a list of your currently open buffers, the command C-x C-b will present you with a comprehensive view, allowing you to select your next target with precision.

When it comes to editing text and code, essential commands such as C-k (to kill or delete the line), C-y (to yank or paste text), and M-w (to copy or "kill" the selected region without deleting it) form a set of foundational skills that every Emacs user should master. These editing commands ensure that you can manipulate text swiftly, akin to the control an archer has over their bow, allowing for precision adjustments on the fly.

Learning how to search and replace text is also vital. The command C-s initiates an incremental search, letting you type as you search and highlighting occurrences of the searched term. If you need to replace text, familiarize yourself with M-%, which prompts you for text to replace and allows you to confirm each action mindfully, ensuring that you're not just reacting but engaging thoughtfully with your code.

Using commands to navigate within your code is essential for efficiency. You can use C-v to scroll forward by one screen and M-v to scroll backward. For a more granular approach, utilize C-n (next line) and C-p (previous line) to deftly traverse through your code line by line. If you want to jump to a specific line, M-g g invites you to input a line number directly—much like envisioning your target before releasing an arrow.

In the context of working with functions and definitions, leverage the command M-. to jump to the definition of a function called in your code, while M-, returns you to the previous position—taking advantage of Emacs's understanding of code structures to enhance your navigation flow. This understanding reflects the precision of an archer who knows exactly how to adjust their aim based on their previous shots.

Customization is a core tenet of Emacs, and learning to use the M-x command invokes additional functionalities. This prompt allows you to access a myriad of commands and features; simply typing M-x followed by the command name invokes those functionalities, opening the doors to an expansive world of customization possibilities.

Working with lists and directories has its own set of commands, too; C-x d to initiate Dired mode puts you into a file management interface within Emacs itself. From here, you can navigate your directories, copy or move files, and even start an editing session all from within Emacs, exemplifying the versatility and depth embedded in this environment.

To ensure your interactions within Emacs remain sharp and efficient, remember the essential command for quitting the current buffer with C-x k, while C-x C-c will exit Emacs entirely. These commands serve as the closing moves in your coding session, much like an archer carefully putting their bow away after practice.

Ultimately, mastering these essential Emacs commands empowers you to move fluidly through the editor, handling tasks efficiently while maintaining a meditative focus on your coding. Each command becomes an extension of your thoughts and intentions, allowing you to capture ideas without interruption, thus embodying the practice of a Zen archer positioned to hit their target with clarity and purpose. As you continue to explore Emacs, these commands form the foundation upon which you will build a more complex and sophisticated practice tailored to your needs as a coder.

5.2. The Power of Macros

The utilization of macros in Emacs embodies a powerful tool for coders aiming to enhance their efficiency and streamline their work-flows. Like an experienced Zen archer who has mastered the art of a release, turning repetitive tasks into automated actions allows you to focus on precision and creativity. Macros empower users to record and execute a series of commands, transforming monotonous, repetitive activities into seamless processes that save time and reduce error. Understanding and mastering macros can elevate your coding practice, allowing you to channel your energies where they matter most.

To begin, it's essential to grasp the concept of macros. In Emacs, macros can be recorded to capture every keystroke, enabling you to replay those actions at a later time. This functionality minimizes the need for repetitive manual tasks, allowing you to engage in your coding practice with a clearer focus—much like an archer reducing distractions to achieve maximum concentration. For instance, if you often find yourself performing the same formatting steps on multiple pieces of code, you can record a macro that captures those keystrokes, saving you the trouble each time you need to apply those same actions.

To record a macro, start the process by invoking F3 (or C-x (command). The moment you press this key, Emacs begins to record everything you do until you signal the end of the macro recording. Be mindful as you perform each step; envision your intention behind writing the code as you capture each action. To stop recording, simply hit F4 (or C-x)). At this point, the macro is saved, and you can reel it back into action by pressing F4 again. If you want to run the macro multiple times, you can prefix the command with a numerical argument, which tells Emacs to execute the macro that many times in succession. This not only speeds up your workflow but enriches your coding sessions with the clarity of mindful execution.

Moreover, understanding the way to edit and manage macros is imperative to mastering their functionality. You can view and modify the recorded macro by typing C-x e, allowing you to adjust the recorded actions. If you're unsatisfied with a macro performance, take the opportunity to rethink its design. Just as an archer might review their practice to identify areas for refinement, coders must continually assess and recalibrate the macros they utilize.

It can be advantageous to name and save your macros for future use. By using M-x name-last-kbd-macro, you can give your macro a meaningful title that allows you to refer to it easily later. This step enhances organization and efficiency in your workflow, ensuring that the tools you have developed truly reflect your coding needs and intentions. Once named, you can invoke the macro by calling its defined name via M-x <macro-name>, allowing for easy accessibility during your coding sessions.

While macros delve into automation, be wary of their potential pitfalls. Macros can sometimes introduce complexity if the recorded steps involve actions that are context-sensitive or highly specific to a single case. For instance, a macro that capitalizes every instance of a certain string works seamlessly in one buffer but may behave unexpectedly if applied in another context. The key here is to maintain a reflective approach—ensuring that your use of macros aligns with your intention to preserve clarity and readability throughout your code.

Additionally, consider leveraging Emacs Lisp to extend the power of macros beyond the limiting confines of predefined actions. Emacs Lisp can effectively create more advanced macros that can be reused across projects or integrated into your broader coding framework. By writing a simple function that encapsulates the specific steps you intend to automate, you not only gain versatility in your coding practice but also deepen your proficiency in Emacs Lisp, thereby reinforcing a robust understanding of the Emacs environment as a whole.

Moreover, incorporate the functionality of macros alongside editing modes and collaborative tools. In team environments, for instance, provisioning your macros to perform necessary formatting or code structure changes ensures consistency across codebases, signaling collective commitment to best practices in coding. Much like a team of archers shares techniques and aims for accuracy, coders can employ macros to embody collective standards in their collaborative projects.

Ultimately, the practice of using macros in Emacs is about enriching your coding experience with intention and efficiency. These powerful automated tools can transform mundane tasks into moments of flowing creativity, allowing you to focus on the intricacies of your code rather than becoming bogged down by repetitive mechanics. Harnessing the power of macros equips you with additional time and clarity, reminiscent of a Zen archer directing their energy towards the essence of the shot, ultimately honing both skill and artistry.

As you delve deeper into the capabilities of Emacs macros, let your coding sessions evolve into a dance of mindfulness, where every keystroke resonates with intent and every project becomes a target aimed with focus and precision. By mastering the art of macros, not only do you enhance your productivity, but you also cultivate a disciplined coding practice that embraces the spirit of the Zen archer.

5.3. Exploring Emacs Modes

Exploring the various modes within Emacs is akin to understanding the different techniques and strategies available to a Zen archer as they prepare for diverse targets and circumstances. Emacs modes are a powerful feature that dramatically alter the way you interact with the environment, streamlining your coding process and enhancing your overall experience. In this comprehensive exploration, we will dive deep into the customization and utilization of both major and minor modes, equipping you with the tools needed to optimize your workflow effectively.

At its core, Emacs operates within the concepts of major and minor modes. Each mode is designed to tailor the editor's functionality to specific tasks, languages, or workflows, offering a customized experience that resonates with efficient coding practices. Understanding how these modes work and how to manipulate them to your advantage is crucial to mastering the Emacs environment.

Major modes serve as the primary context for coding within Emacs. They define the syntax highlighting, indentation rules, key bindings, and even the overall behavior of the text editor for specific file types. For example, there are major modes specifically designed for languages like Python, JavaScript, and C++, among many others. Each major mode comes equipped with its tailored functionalities, enhancing your coding experience and ensuring that you interact with the code with the proper context in mind.

To switch between major modes, you can use the command `M-x` followed by the mode name, such as `python-mode`, `js-mode`, or `ruby-mode`. This command invokes the associated functionalities, such as highlighting syntax, offering language-specific commands, and facilitating interactive features like code completion. This flexibility is similar to an archer adjusting their stance and strategy depending on the distance to the target—mode adjustments enable you to effectively engage with the unique characteristics of your code.

In addition to switching major modes, Emacs allows the flexibility to configure how these modes function. You may choose to set specific options for each mode in your Emacs configuration file (init.el). For instance, you might want to enable or customize automatic indentation settings or syntax checking for specific programming languages. Consider incorporating snippets of code such as:

```
(add-hook 'python-mode-hook
          (lambda ()
            (setq indent-tabs-mode nil)
            (setq python-indent 4)))
```

This example configures Python mode to use spaces instead of tabs and sets the indentations to four spaces, ensuring a consistent coding experience.

Minor modes, on the other hand, add additional functionalities that can operate alongside any major mode. These modes enhance your coding environment without fundamentally altering its core behavior. For example, the auto-fill-mode allows for automatic line breaking at a certain character limit, keeping your code tidy and presentable. To enable a minor mode, you also use M-x followed by the desired mode name, such as auto-fill-mode or flyspell-mode for spell checking in text buffers.

The beauty of minor modes lies in their ability to coexist peacefully with major modes, thus allowing for extensive customization of your coding experience. An archer using various techniques based on specific scenarios can be likened to a coder seamlessly integrating multiple minor modes depending on the task at hand. To get the most out of minor modes, you can create specific key bindings that can be activated based on your preferences. For instance, if you find that certain functionalities are indispensable for your workflow, setting:

```
(global-set-key (kbd "C-c f") 'auto-fill-mode)
```

can provide quick access, allowing you to toggle automatic line breaking effortlessly.

As you explore modes, it is worthwhile to engage with the vast library of Emacs packages available, as many offer modes that are community-driven and specifically designed to enhance functionality for particular tasks. The package manager in Emacs facilitates this process by allowing you to install, configure, and update various packages that can provide tailored major and minor modes based on your coding preferences. Utilizing packages like `company-mode` for autocompletion, `magit` for Git integration, and `projectile` for project management can exponentially improve your productivity, much like an archer using optimized equipment for better accuracy.

Engaging with the Emacs community can also help uncover new modes or variants that align with your workflow. By participating in forums, reading documentation, or joining discussions, you can gather insights on the best practices for utilizing modes effectively. This collaborative approach enables you to refine your skills and techniques, akin to archers training together to share tips and enhance each other's accuracy and performance.

Additionally, taking the initiative to create your own custom modes or modify existing ones can amplify the benefits of Emacs. For users looking to tailor their environment even further, consider using Emacs Lisp to define specific functionalities or behaviors that align with your needs. This level of customization not only personalizes your workflow but also deepens your understanding of how Emacs operates under the hood, offering you more control over your coding experience.

In summary, the exploration of Emacs modes—their customization and utilization—opens a door to an enriched coding practice. Just as a Zen archer adapts their technique to the target, mastering modes in Emacs allows you to tailor your environment to suit your particular coding style and tasks. By leveraging the strengths of major and minor modes, collaborating with the community, and infusing your personal touch into your setup, you will enhance your workflow significantly, allowing you to hit the bullseye with your coding endeavors consistently. Embrace the journey of exploring and mastering

Emacs modes, and you will cultivate a mindful and effective coding practice that harmonizes with the principles of Zen.

5.4. Debugging with Precision

In the world of coding, precision in debugging is as vital as the steady hand of a Zen archer aiming for the bullseye. This subchapter explores the nuanced landscape of debugging within Emacs, equipping you with powerful tools and techniques for quick identification and resolution of coding issues. By incorporating precision into your debugging practices, you can enhance your workflow, reduce frustration, and approach errors with a calm, focused mindset that embodies the principles of Zen.

The foundation of effective debugging lies in understanding the tools available within Emacs. At the core of these tools is the built-in edebug, an interactive debugger for Emacs Lisp code, which allows users to source errors and understand code flow deeply. By setting breakpoints in your code, you can pause execution at crucial moments, analyze variable states, and navigate through the stack, akin to an archer stepping back to assess their stance and the surrounding conditions before drawing their bow. To activate edebug, use the command M-x edebug-defun on the function you wish to troubleshoot. This command turns the function into an edebug-enabled version, allowing you to step through the code when run.

Utilizing pop-to-buffer when an error occurs is also essential in your debugging arsenal. Emacs buffers hold the output of execution and errors, affording an opportunity to review messages or logs relevant to your code. By focusing on the error messages presented in these buffers, you can quickly zero in on the line or section of code that triggered an issue, fostering the analytical mindset necessary for debugging. Just as an archer mentally notes their misses and adjusts their form, programmers must absorb these errors and translate them into actionable insights.

Beyond edebug, Emacs supports other prominent tools like flycheck, which provides on-the-fly syntax checking as you code. The gentle nudges provided by flycheck highlight problematic lines, allowing you to take corrective action immediately. This functionality parallels the way a coach might guide an archer to correct their stance in real-time, ensuring they hit their mark with precision. By integrating flycheck into your workflow, you cultivate an environment in which errors are caught early and addressed before they compound into greater challenges.

Another aspect of debugging involves the proper use of Emacs's *Messages* buffer. This buffer serves as a log of commands and error messages, acting as a trail of breadcrumbs leading you back to the source of the problem. With the command C-h e, you can open the **Messages** buffer and review its content for insight into prior operations, errors, and the results of executed commands. This practice cultivates a reflective approach, encouraging you to consider past actions in the same manner that an archer evaluates their path to improve future efforts.

In addition to using Emacs tools, adopting a structured approach toward debugging can further enhance your effectiveness. Begin by clearly identifying the problem statement; articulate what the expected behavior of the code should be versus what it is currently doing. This process not only provides clarity but lays the groundwork for targeted troubleshooting, much like an archer focusing on specific techniques to improve accuracy.

Next, isolate the problem area by systematically commenting out segments of code to narrow down the issue. This step is akin to simplifying your stance to check for correctness—by removing potential distractions, you can focus solely on the current target. Slowly reintroducing code segments can help pinpoint the precise cause of the error, turning a chaotic debugging session into a focused inquiry.

Throughout the debugging process, maintaining a balanced mindset is crucial. Just as the Zen archer practices calmness to avoid erratic shooting, entering the debugging space with a composed attitude can significantly increase the likelihood of successful resolutions. If you find yourself frustrated or overwhelmed, take a mindful pause—step away, breathe, and return with a fresh perspective. Often, a brief retreat allows for new insights to emerge, letting your subconscious mind address unresolved problems.

Additionally, consider embracing collaboration during debugging sessions. Much like an archer benefits from input from fellow team members, coding can greatly improve when shared. Discussing issues with peers can bring new ideas and methodologies to the forefront, enhancing your approach to finding solutions. Engaging in pair programming or code reviews provides the added benefit of diverse perspectives, fostering a communal spirit that embodies the principles of Zen.

Lastly, remember that debugging is a skill that develops with practice. As you continue to confront and resolve coding errors, you will cultivate a rhythm to your debugging practice, becoming increasingly adept at navigating complexities with confidence and focus. Each successful debugging session reinforces the mindset necessary to tackle future errors, much like a Zen archer strengthening their resolve with every shot taken.

In conclusion, debugging with precision in Emacs is an art that mirrors the disciplined practice of a Zen archer aiming for the bullseye. By leveraging the built-in tools of Emacs, adopting structured methodologies, and maintaining a calm mindset during the debugging process, you can transform potential frustrations into learning opportunities. With each resolved issue, you not only sharpen your coding skills but also cultivate an understanding of your code that drives you towards mastery in your craft. Embrace the debugging journey with clarity and intention, and let your coding practice achieve the depths of precision that do justice to the true spirit of Zen.

5.5. Version Control Integration

Version control is a fundamental aspect of modern software development that allows teams to manage changes to source code over time. In the context of Emacs, version control integration, particularly with

Git, can enhance your coding workflow significantly. By utilizing various Emacs packages and built-in support for Git, you can stream-line version management and collaborate effortlessly with your team, embodying the same focused precision of a Zen archer aiming for the target.

To begin harnessing the power of version control in Emacs, it's essential first to familiarize yourself with the basics of Git. Git is a distributed version control system that tracks changes in your files, allowing multiple developers to work concurrently without conflict. Understanding core concepts like repositories, commits, branches, and merging will provide the foundation necessary for effective inte-gration within Emacs.

One of the most powerful tools available to Emacs users for Git integration is `magit`. Magit offers an intuitive user interface to Git, leveraging the Emacs environment while providing a seamless work-flow for executing Git commands. To get started with Magit, install it through Emacs's package manager by invoking `M-x package-install RET magit RET`, and then add the following to your Emacs configuration file to activate it:

```
(require 'magit)
```

Upon installation, you can open a Magit status buffer with `M-x magit-status`. This command presents a comprehensive overview of your Git repository, showing staged changes, unstaged changes, branches, and recent commits—all located in one easily navigable interface. Navigating these options is akin to the Zen archer surveying the landscape before taking a shot; you can reflect on your code's current state before deciding how to proceed.

Magit significantly simplifies the process of staging and committing changes. Instead of using the command line, you can stage files inter-actively by moving to the desired file in the Magit status buffer and pressing the s key. Committing changes is just as effortless; press c followed by c again, and you'll be prompted to enter a commit mes-sage in a dedicated buffer. This built-in functionality allows coders to focus on their tasks, emphasizing clarity and intention in their actions —as the Zen archer does before taking aim.

Branch management is another critical aspect of version control that Magit handles with elegance. Utilizing b in the Magit status buffer, you can create new branches, switch between them, and merge changes with ease. When you create a new branch, it encourages you to isolate features or fixes, embodying the disciplined separation of concerns. Merging branches, especially after collaborating with fellow developers, is made simple: switch to the branch you want to merge changes into, use m from Magit, and select the branch you want to merge. This efficiency reduces the friction of coordination and enhances collaborative development.

Imagine working in a team on a feature branch, where multiple developers contribute independently. When it's time to merge their work, Magit's visual diff tools become invaluable. When conflicts arise during merging—an inevitable aspect of collaborative coding—Magit will highlight the conflicting sections of code. It allows you to review each conflicting change side by side, enhancing your decision-making process. Undoing changes or reverting commits is just a keystroke away while armed with the mindset of a focused archer, allowing you to act decisively and purposefully.

An excellent practice when working with version control, particularly in collaborative settings, is to use commit messages that convey intent clearly, akin to a Zen archer's focus on each movement. Writing descriptive commit messages summarizing the change facilitates understanding across the team and provides clarity when reviewing the project's history. Adopt a habit to write your commit messages in the imperative form—this convention underscores the action the commit represents, making it more impactful for your team members.

In addition to Magit, several other Emacs packages can complement your version control practices. For example, vc-mode, which is built into Emacs, provides basic version control functionalities, offering a simplified interface for managing multiple version control systems like Git, Mercurial, and SVN. Using vc commands, you can quickly access or check the status of your files without relying solely on external processes. This flexibility enriches your Emacs environment, enabling you to respond to changes swiftly.

To truly embrace version control in your workflow, make it a core part of your development process. Regularly commit your changes, take advantage of branching to manage new features, and use merging to incorporate collaborative efforts. Just as an archer practices consistently to improve their aim, regular engagement with version control reinforces your skills, ensuring that you become proficient with managing changes effectively.

Additionally, consider building a habit of reflecting on your codebase's history. Regularly review past commits and branches to evaluate the evolution of your project. Utilize Magit's log functionality with l for both the branch history and the reflog, offering insights into how your project has developed over time. This introspective approach mirrors the reflective nature of Zen practice, encouraging continuous learning and adaptation.

In summary, integrating version control within Emacs, particularly through tools like Magit, fundamentally enhances your coding workflow. By ensuring that the principles of version control are interwoven into your practice, you create an environment conducive to collaboration and mindfulness. As you navigate the complexities of your code with the clarity and focus of a Zen archer, you'll find that each commit, branch, and merge is an intentional step toward achieving not just successful projects, but a deeper mastery of your craft. Embrace version control integration, ensuring that each coding session mirrors the precision and attentiveness that lie at the heart of both Zen and successful software development.

6. The Zen Coding Techniques

6.1. Coding with Mindfulness

Coding with Mindfulness is an approach that seeks to weave the principles of mindfulness into our daily programming practices, allowing for a more thoughtful, intentional coding experience. In the fast-paced world of software development, where deadlines loom and distractions abound, the practice of mindfulness offers a pathway to reconnect with our work, cultivate focus, and enhance the quality of our coding.

At its heart, coding with mindfulness is about bringing awareness to the act of coding itself. It encourages us to slow down our thought processes and engage fully in the task at hand. By consciously dedicating ourselves to our coding sessions, we create space to explore the nuances of our work and grasp its intricacies. Mindfulness prompts us to ask, "What is my purpose in this moment?" Every line of code we write can become a deliberate choice rather than an automated response. This transforms coding from a mechanized task into a mindful art form.

The practice begins with setting the stage for mindful coding. Consider your environment and how it can influence your state of mind. A cluttered workspace often has a direct impact on your ability to focus and think clearly. Tidy your coding area, ensuring that only essential tools and materials are at hand. This mirrors the Zen practice of simplicity, where removing distractions can allow for a clearer flow of thought. Additionally, pay attention to your physical comfort; an ergonomic chair, appropriate desk height, and good lighting can enhance your experience, allowing you to fully engage in your work.

Another pivotal aspect of coding with mindfulness is the intentional use of breath. Breathing is a powerful anchor that can help ground us during moments of stress or confusion. Before you dive into a coding session, take a moment to focus on your breath. Inhale deeply for a count of four, hold for a moment, and then exhale for the same count. As you do this, allow any lingering thoughts about external pressures to dissipate, returning your focus to the present moment. This practice not only calms the mind but can also rejuvenate your mental clarity, allowing you to code with greater intention.

While coding, it's crucial to maintain awareness of your thought patterns and emotional responses. As you encounter challenges—be it a bug that needs squashing or an unfamiliar library—practice observing your feelings without judgment. Notice any frustration or impatience that arises. Instead of reacting impulsively, acknowledge these emotions and allow them to pass. Choose to approach the challenge with curiosity rather than dread. Each obstacle is an opportunity for growth; viewing them through the lens of mindfulness transforms stress into discovery, making the coding journey one of continuous learning.

Incorporating regular breaks into your coding routine is essential for maintaining mindfulness. The Pomodoro Technique—a method involving focused work sessions followed by short breaks—can help establish a balanced rhythm. Set a timer for 25 minutes of focused coding, then take a 5-minute pause. During these breaks, step away from your screen, stretch, hydrate, or engage in short mindfulness exercises. This cycle of work and rest reflects the Zen principle of balance and allows your mind to rejuvenate, enhancing overall productivity and awareness.

As you progress through your coding tasks, cultivate a sense of gratitude for the process. Take a moment to appreciate the act of creation —transforming lines of code into a functional program. Celebrate small victories such as successfully implementing a new feature or solving a challenging problem. This practice, akin to savoring each shot taken by an archer, fosters a positive atmosphere around your work, reinforcing the joy of coding and cultivating mindfulness throughout the process.

By being present in our coding practices, we not only produce better code but also nurture our well-being and growth as coders. The journey of coding with mindfulness cultivates patience, empathy, and a sense of connectedness to both our work and the wider coding community. Engaging with others mindfully in code reviews, collaborative pair programming, and discussions allows us to share insights and foster a supportive environment.

In conclusion, coding with mindfulness invites us to slow down, connect with our work, and appreciate the journey we embark upon in our coding endeavors. Through intentional practices, we learn to navigate challenges with grace and transform potential chaos into opportunities for insight and growth. This approach invites a sense of calm and purpose into our coding routines, allowing us to become not just proficient developers, but mindful creators in the digital realm, hitting the coding bullseye with intention and clarity.

6.2. Zen in Error Handling

Error handling in the coding realm shares similarities with the art of archery, where each miss serves as an opportunity for growth and insight. Just as a Zen archer practices self-reflection after a shot, learning from each error in coding can enhance performance and cultivate resilience. Approaching errors with a calm, focused mindset allows developers to transform frustrations into valuable learning experiences, ultimately leading to better code and greater mastery of the craft.

The first step in effective error handling is to embrace a mindset of curiosity rather than blame. When an error arises, it is easy to feel frustration and self-doubt, akin to an archer missing a target and contemplating their worth as a marksman. However, adopting a curious perspective invites analysis and understanding of the underlying cause. Instead of reacting with negativity, pause and acknowledge the error without judgment. This approach encourages a reflective attitude, allowing for deeper investigation into what caused the issue, much like an archer assessing their stance and technique after a disappointing shot.

Once the initial shock of the error subsides, create a systematic approach to diagnosing the issue. Begin by reproducing the error, as this will provide context and insights into the conditions under which it occurs. For example, if a function behaves unexpectedly, determine whether the issue arises consistently or under specific circumstances. Use debugging tools, such as breakpoints in an integrated debugger or print statements, to trace the flow of execution and observe variable states. This process mirrors the archery practice of checking equipment and adjusting one's technique to correct misalignment. The clearer your understanding of the error, the more effectively you can address it.

In the spirit of Zen, documentation and reflection are crucial components of error handling. Keep a record of common errors you encounter along with their resolutions. Creating a "debug log" can serve as a personalized reference guide, a sort of toolkit that future-proof your coding journey. Each entry should include the error message, the context in which it occurred, and the steps taken to resolve it. This documentation not only helps you remember solutions but also serves as a reminder of your development as a coder—a tangible representation of how each mistake contributed to your growth.

Moreover, during the resolution process, maintain a focus on clarity and simplicity. Aim to refactor code when appropriate, removing unnecessary complexity that could lead to future errors. This mirrors the Zen principle of simplicity, which emphasizes quality and purpose. Clear and maintainable code reduces the likelihood of errors, fostering a calm coding environment that encourages continued learning and improvement. As a Zen archer emphasizes form and grace in every shot, so too should you prioritize the elegance and clarity of your code.

It's also essential to foster a culture of open communication and collaboration when facing errors as part of a team. Just as archers sometimes train together, coders benefit tremendously from sharing insights and support. Encourage a non-toxic atmosphere where team members feel safe discussing errors and uncertainties. Engaging in code reviews and pair programming sessions fosters a collective learning environment—enabling each member to share strategies for resolving issues. This community-oriented approach not only strengthens the team but also elevates the quality of code produced collectively.

Further enhancing your error handling can be achieved through the implementation of robust testing frameworks. By adopting a test-driven development (TDD) mindset, you not only catch errors earlier in the coding process but also build confidence in your codebase over time. Define tests for your functions before implementation, ensuring that as you write code, you do so with a clear understanding of the expected outcomes. This practice allows for proactive error identification and creates a safety net that fosters clarity, much like a Zen archer relying on their disciplined practice to instill confidence in their skills.

Finally, celebrate your successes in overcoming errors and view them as milestones in your coding journey. Each resolved issue is not only a marker of improved code but evidence of your growth as a developer. By celebrating these achievements—whether through personal reflection or sharing with your team—you reinforce a positive mindset that diminishes the fear of errors. Embrace the understanding that errors are not adversaries but rather stepping stones on your path toward mastery and excellence in coding.

In summary, Zen in error handling entails a mindful approach to addressing bugs and issues in your code. Embrace curiosity, create documentation, foster collaboration, prioritize clarity, utilize testing strategies, and celebrate your successes. By transforming errors into opportunities for growth, you embody the principles of a Zen archer —effortlessly learning from each shot while cultivating grace, precision, and resilience in your coding practice. Let this mindful approach guide you in navigating the complexities of coding, empowering you to consistently hit your targets and achieve coding excellence.

6.3. The Art of Code Review

The art of code review is recognition of the subtle balance between written code as a technical artifact and the dynamic exchange of insights, improvements, and collaborative growth among peers. Just as an archer meticulously examines their technique and seeks feedback from their peers, coders must cultivate a spirit of openness and humility in reviewing code. This section will explore effective strategies to conduct and participate in code reviews, transforming a routine task into a harmonious and enriching practice.

The foundation of successful code reviews starts with establishing a culture of respect and constructive criticism. It is imperative to create an environment where feedback is taken as an opportunity for growth rather than as a personal critique. This atmosphere parallels the supportive community of archers, where feedback is rooted in shared goals for improvement. Encourage team members to approach each review with the mindset of enhancing the codebase and fostering collaboration rather than merely pointing out flaws.

To kick off a code review effectively, frame the discussion around the objectives of the code being reviewed. Start the process by articulating the purpose and intended outcome of the code. This clarity of intent helps both the reviewer and the author align on key aspects of the implementation. Just as an archer studies the target before taking aim, reviewers must examine not only the code itself but the context in which it operates. Understanding why certain decisions were made provides insight into the design and thought processes behind the implementation.

As you engage in a code review, it is important to balance critique with acknowledgment. Highlight what is working well before diving into suggestions for improvement. This positive reinforcement encourages the author and instills a sense of accomplishment and motivation. Consider using the "sandwich" approach—start with commendation, insert constructive feedback in the middle, and end with an encouraging note. This alignment fosters collaboration and keeps the atmosphere light and supportive, much like a team of archers celebrating each other's successes on the range.

Constructive feedback should be specific, actionable, and framed positively. Instead of saying, "This part is confusing," try reframing it to "Consider adding comments here for clarity about this logic." Such specificity provides clearer direction and shows consideration for the author's learning journey. Reviewers should strive to make their comments insightful, illustrating the reasoning behind suggested changes. Sharing references to coding best practices, guidelines, or resources encourages broader learning and growth in connection to the feedback provided.

Moreover, reviewing code involves not only understanding the syntax but recognizing how well the implementation adheres to established coding standards and patterns. Encourage conversations around naming conventions, code structure, and design patterns that enhance maintainability. A team's collective adherence to these principles ensures that the codebase remains clean and understandable for both current and future contributors. Much like an archer refining their stance for optimal performance, fostering best practices within the code reinforces quality.

It is also important to establish a sense of ownership and accountability within the code review process. Authors should view feedback as a collaborative effort focused on improving the collective output rather than placing blame. Encourage team members to actively engage with feedback for clarification if needed, and foster discussion around proposed changes. This interaction mimics the focused dialogue among archers analyzing potential adjustments to their technique, enhancing group learning through shared experiences.

One effective method to enhance the code review process is through the use of visual tools that provide historical context. Utilizing platforms like GitHub, GitLab, or Bitbucket enhances clarity during reviews by allowing team members to track changes, comment directly on lines of code, and see the evolution of the project over time. This ability to visualize changes serves as a helpful reminder of progress and fosters transparency in the review process, akin to an archer keeping track of their shots over time.

Additionally, consider integrating tools that automate routine aspects of code reviews. Tools like linters or continuous integration systems can flag issues prior to the review process, allowing reviewers to focus on higher-level discussions around logic, design, and architecture rather than syntax errors. Automated testing also ensures that feedback can be contextualized within the broader functionality of the project, reflecting the careful preparation an archer undertakes before each shot.

As a health check for the review process, it is beneficial to establish clear guidelines around code review expectations. Define how long code reviews should typically take, what aspects should be prioritized, and how feedback should be delivered. Such guidelines create consistency within the team and ensure that code reviews become a productive and efficient process. Team members should feel comfortable setting boundaries, ensuring they allocate sufficient time and resources for thorough code evaluations.

Finally, to close the code review loop, encourage a culture of continuous learning and reflection on the experience. After a series of code reviews, take the time to discuss successes and challenges in a team retrospective. This practice allows team members to share their experiences with the code review process, highlighting what worked well and what could be enhanced. This sense of reflection serves not only to improve the immediate process but also to cultivate a culture of growth over time.

In conclusion, the art of code review embodies the essence of collaboration, growth, and technical excellence. By fostering an environment of mutual respect, constructive feedback, and continuous learning, team members can evolve their coding practices collectively. Approaching code reviews as opportunities to refine skills, share knowledge, and build a supportive coding community transforms a routine exercise into a vital aspect of development. Through these practices, coders become adept at hitting their targets with purpose and clarity, enhancing both individual and team success in the coding journey.

6.4. Refactoring: The Zen Way

Refactoring, often considered an essential practice in software development, aligns closely with the principles of Zen—clarity, simplicity, and intentionality. Just as a Zen archer refines their technique to improve accuracy and precision, so too should a coder embrace refactoring as a means to elevate the quality and maintainability of their code. This section delves into the art of refactoring through a Zen lens, offering insights into how to approach this practice mindfully and effectively.

At the heart of refactoring is the commitment to improve existing code without altering its external behavior. This practice is not merely about making code work; it's about enhancing its structure, readability, and performance. Much like a Zen practitioner who seeks to refine their thoughts and actions, the coder must embrace a mindset aimed at cultivating clarity and efficiency. To refactor effectively, start by assessing the current state of your code. Identify areas that feel cumbersome, duplicative, or unnecessarily complex. Treat this initial examination like an archer evaluating their form—honest reflection is key to understanding where improvements are needed.

Once you've identified code that requires refactoring, set clear objectives for what you hope to achieve with each change. These goals might include improving code readability, reducing complexity, or removing redundancy. By defining your intentions upfront, you embody the Zen value of purposeful action. For example, if a function has grown too long and convoluted, consider breaking it down into smaller, more manageable pieces that encapsulate single responsibilities. This practice mirrors the Zen principle of simplicity—stripping away layers of excess to unveil the elegance inherent in concise, focused functions.

As you embark on the refactoring journey, embrace the notion of small, incremental changes. Just as an archer practices with a gradual increase in difficulty, apply the same philosophy to your code. Make single, focused changes, and run tests at each step to validate that functionality remains intact. This iterative approach minimizes the risk of introducing errors, fostering a sense of control and assurance akin to the steady pull of the bowstring before a shot.

During refactoring, documentation plays a vital role in preserving context and clarity. As you modify functions or change variable names, update comments and documentation to reflect these changes. This practice helps maintain aligned understanding among all involved in the project and establishes a reference point for the future, ensuring that your work continues to resonate even as the code evolves. Just as an archer maintains a practice journal, tracking progress and insights, keeping detailed documentation cultivates a habit of reflection that enhances personal growth as a developer.

Incorporate the principles of code readability and style consistency throughout the refactoring process. Strive for a visually clean and organized structure so that your code becomes instrumentally readable —an aspect that often gets sidelined in the rush to deliver functionality. Use consistent naming conventions and adhere to established style guides that resonate within the language community. Each line of code should reflect intention and clarity, as has been cultivated by the mindful archer in their aim.

Additionally, pair programming can amplify growth and insights during refactoring. Inviting a colleague to engage in the process brings diverse perspectives that may lead to improvements you might not have considered alone. As with Zen archery, where practitioners may analyze each other's form for subtle tweaks and enhancements, collaborative coding fosters a climate of shared learning and collective success. Communication and transparency throughout the process enable team members to remain aligned on objectives and foster greater understanding of the codebase.

Moreover, regular code reviews should be integrated into your workflow to support ongoing refactoring efforts. Setting up regular intervals to assess code collectively provides opportunities to spot inconsistencies, complexity, or areas lacking clarity. This practice mirrors the iterative nature of Zen training—continued reflection and input lead to continuous improvement as coders support each other in reaching shared coding goals.

As part of developing your refactoring practice, it is essential to recognize the emotional weight that accompanies changes to established code. Let go of attachment to initial implementations; acknowledge that evolution is part of the coding journey. Much like an archer who might need to adjust their technique, understanding that refactoring is integral to producing better code fosters openness to change. Seek balance between confidence in your original work and the clarity that comes from transformative growth.

In conclusion, refactoring embodies a Zen practice that encourages clarity, simplicity, and focus in coding. By approaching code with a mindset of continual improvement, defining clear objectives, adopting incremental changes, maintaining robust documentation, and promoting collaboration, you cultivate a refined and effective coding environment. Engage with the practice of refactoring not merely as a technical necessity, but as an artistic endeavor that enhances the experience of coding while nurturing your growth as a developer. Embrace each refactoring session as an opportunity to hone your skills, hit your targets with precision, and embody the spirit of the Zen archer in your work.

6.5. Continuous Learning and Adaptation

Continuous learning and adaptation are fundamental principles deeply rooted in both Zen philosophy and effective coding practices. Much like the Zen archer who continuously hones their skills, striving for improvement with each shot, coders too must embrace a mindset of lifelong learning to navigate the ever-evolving landscape of technology. The journey of coding is not a destination; rather, it is an ongoing process of exploration, growth, and evolution, driven by an intrinsic desire to improve and adapt.

To fully grasp the importance of continuous learning in coding, let us first acknowledge that technology and programming languages are in a constant state of flux. New languages, frameworks, libraries, and paradigms emerge rapidly, reshaping the way developers approach problem-solving. In this dynamic environment, reliance on past knowledge alone can quickly become outdated. The ability to learn new skills and adapt to changes is crucial for remaining relevant in the field. By cultivating a habit of lifelong learning, coders can ensure that their skill sets remain sharp and adaptable, much like an archer practicing regularly to refine their aim and techniques.

A powerful approach to continuous learning is to adopt a mindset that embraces curiosity and openness. Instead of viewing challenges as obstacles, consider them opportunities for growth. When faced with a problem or unfamiliar technology, allow yourself to explore and experiment rather than feeling disheartened by initial failures. This paradigm shift fosters resilience and encourages a playful approach to learning, enabling you to uncover innovative solutions and deepen your understanding of complex concepts.

Another significant aspect of continuous learning in coding is the practice of reflection. After completing a project or learning a new technology, take time to analyze the experience. What worked well, and what could have been improved? Reflecting on your experiences allows you to codify your understanding and apply those lessons to future projects. Additionally, documenting your reflections in a learning journal can provide valuable insights over time, serving as a record of your growth as a developer.

Collaboration and engagement with the coding community also play a crucial role in facilitating continuous learning. Engaging with peers, mentors, and thought leaders exposes you to diverse perspectives and new ideas. Participate in coding meetups, online forums, or workshops, where knowledge exchange and collaborative problem-solving flourish. Sharing your own experiences, lessons learned, and challenges faced creates an atmosphere of support and collective learning—much like archers training together, improving their skills through shared practice and feedback.

Furthermore, leveraging the vast array of online resources can accelerate your learning. From tutorials, open-source projects, webinars, and online courses to documentation, blogs, and community forums, the wealth of accessible knowledge online is immense. When diving into a new language or framework, prioritize self-directed exploration, utilizing these resources as tools for deeper understanding. This proactive approach to learning empowers you to shape your educational journey, ensuring that you're equipped with the tools and knowledge necessary to tackle new challenges confidently.

Adaptability, as an extension of continuous learning, is equally essential. In coding, adaptability refers to the ability to approach new situations with a flexible mindset. When project requirements change or new technologies arise, being able to pivot and adjust your strategies is crucial for success. Develop a comfort level with ambiguity and embrace the unknown. This mindset allows you to respond effectively to change, fostering creativity and innovation while ensuring that you remain open to new opportunities.

Integrating regular learning routines into your schedule can also enhance your continuous learning habit. Just as dedication to archery practice leads to mastery, setting aside time for coding practice—be it daily or weekly—ensures that learning becomes a priority. Create a study plan that encompasses a mix of formal learning, personal projects, and collaborative engagements. Establish goals that encourage you to explore new concepts, sharpen existing skills, and apply your knowledge in meaningful ways.

Lastly, recognize that continuous learning and adaptation are not purely intellectual pursuits. They are deeply intertwined with personal growth and self-awareness. Cultivating a supportive mindset —a blend of patience, persistence, and compassion towards yourself —allows you to navigate the inevitable ups and downs of learning. Embrace the understanding that mistakes are an integral part of the journey, each one offering valuable insights that contribute to your development as both a coder and an individual.

In conclusion, continuous learning and adaptation are essential principles that underpin success in coding. By fostering a mindset of curiosity and resilience, engaging with the community, leveraging available resources, and maintaining adaptability, you can navigate the ever-changing landscape of technology with confidence. As you embark on your coding journey, strive to cultivate an approach that reflects the spirit of the Zen archer—one that values growth, embraces challenges, and always aims for improvement. Ultimately, by committing to a lifelong learning process, you will not only enhance your technical skills but also deepen your connection to the craft, achieving mastery that resonates far beyond the screen.

7. Creating an Emacs Workflow

7.1. Workflow Foundations

Workflow Foundations in Emacs encapsulate the essential principles, practices, and tools that enable coders to achieve efficiency, clarity, and intent within their coding environment. Just as an archer practices with discipline to enhance their performance, establishing a strong workflow foundation in Emacs serves as the bedrock upon which your coding journey can thrive. This section will guide you through the key components of an effective Emacs workflow, emphasizing the importance of structure, reflection, and adaptability.

The first element of a solid workflow foundation is the configuration of your Emacs environment. This involves personalizing your setup through the `init.el` or `.emacs` configuration files, where you define functions, set defaults, and load plugins that resonate with your specific needs as a coder. Like an archer tuning their bow before practice, customizing your Emacs environment ensures that the workspace is built to enhance focus and productivity. Start by selecting a theme that is visually appealing and easy on the eyes, opting for a color scheme that helps maintain mental clarity during long coding sessions.

Keybindings form another crucial aspect of your Emacs workflow. These shortcuts transform your interaction with Emacs from a laborious series of movements into a fluid dance of keystrokes. Just as an archer practices their stance and draw to achieve precision, mastering keybindings allows you to navigate and execute commands with ease. Spend time configuring your keybindings to reflect your workflow preferences, creating shortcuts that give you direct access to frequently used features, commands, or snippets.

Moreover, effective use of modes within Emacs enhances the workflow by adapting the editor's behavior to suit different programming tasks. Emacs major modes serve as context-specific environments that enable you to write and edit code efficiently. For instance, you can use `python-mode` for Python development and `js-mode` for JavaScript.

Familiarize yourself with the major modes relevant to your work, customizing their settings to fit your preferences. Minor modes, such as `flycheck` for real-time syntax checking or `rainbow-delimiters` for visually differentiating parentheses, further enrich your experience by providing additional features that simplify coding tasks.

Task management is essential in a balanced workflow and can be effectively implemented through tools like `org-mode`. Org-mode facilitates project management, task tracking, and documentation within Emacs. Utilizing org files to organize thoughts, code snippets, and tasks provides a cohesive structure for your workflow. Encoding your tasks using headings and organizing them hierarchically mimics the structured approach of an archer's training regimen. Create to-do lists, schedule recurring tasks, and make annotations directly in your org files, allowing Emacs to be a single source of truth for your coding endeavors.

Additionally, the concept of streams and workflows in coding emphasizes the importance of transitioning between projects and tasks. Emacs excels in buffer management, allowing you to maintain multiple files and projects simultaneously. Learn to navigate buffers quickly with commands such as `C-x b` to switch between them fluidly, minimizing context-switching distractions. Use macros to automate repetitive tasks, decreasing cognitive load and enhancing your efficiency.

Building a foundation also involves continuous reflection and iteration on your practices. After completing significant projects or milestones, take time to examine your process. Reflect on what went well and what challenges you encountered. This introspection allows you to identify areas for improvement—akin to an archer reviewing their performance to refine their technique. Establish a habit of reviewing your workflow regularly, ensuring that it evolves alongside your growth as a coder.

Embracing the principle of adaptability is vital. As you advance in your coding journey, your workflow may need to change to embrace new technologies, languages, or methodologies. Continuously seek opportunities for improvement by staying informed about the latest developments in the Emacs community and beyond. Experiment with new plugins or techniques that align with your goals, remaining flexible to the ever-changing landscape of software development.

Finally, remember that cultivating a mindful coding workflow is not a solo endeavor. Engage with your peers and the broader Emacs community to share experiences, insights, and strategies. Participate in coding collaborations, forums, and discussions that emphasize collective learning. This connection reinforces the sense of purpose behind your work, much like a community of archers training together to enhance their skills and camaraderie.

In conclusion, the foundations of a productive Emacs workflow encompass thoughtful configuration, mastery of tools and techniques, reflective practices, and adaptation to change. By establishing a strong groundwork for your coding journey in Emacs, you can approach each project with focus, intent, and clarity, ultimately setting yourself on a path to productive and fulfilling coding experiences. Embrace the spirit of the Zen archer, preparing yourself to hit the bullseye in your coding endeavors, and allow these foundational practices to guide your journey toward mastery.

7.2. The Role of Scheduling in Coding

Scheduling plays a pivotal role in coding, acting as the structural backbone that supports a productive and balanced workflow. Just as archers meticulously plan their training regimens in preparation for competition, coders benefit from intentional scheduling that paves the way for consistent progress, focused concentration, and mindfulness. In this exploration of scheduling in coding, we will discuss strategies for building a meaningful coding schedule that fosters productivity, reflects personal goals, and enhances your overall coding experience.

At the heart of effective scheduling is the cultivation of a routine. A well-defined routine empowers you to allocate time thoughtfully across various coding tasks, allowing for deeper engagement with your work. Start by assessing your current workload and commitments. Consider factors such as deadlines, project complexity, and personal energy levels throughout the day. Once you have a clear understanding of your landscape, you can begin to outline a daily or weekly coding schedule that accommodates these variables.

When structuring your schedule, it can be beneficial to employ techniques such as the Pomodoro Technique, which emphasizes focused work intervals followed by short breaks. For example, designate 25 minutes of uninterrupted coding followed by a 5-minute break. This technique encourages sustained concentration while preventing fatigue, allowing you to maintain a state of flow throughout your coding sessions. As you embody the discipline of an archer aiming for precision, you can apply similar focus to your work.

Intentional breaks are equally crucial in your scheduling strategy. Research has shown that the brain's ability to concentrate diminishes over time, making regular breaks essential for maintaining high levels of productivity. Use these breaks to step away from your workstation, stretch, go for a brief walk, or engage in other activities that promote mental rejuvenation. This conscious interplay between focused work and restorative breaks fosters a balanced routine, mirroring the Zen practice of harmonizing effort with relaxation.

In addition to daily routines, consider the importance of long-term scheduling. Utilize tools like calendars or project management apps to map out larger milestones and deadlines associated with your coding projects. Schedule significant tasks into your calendar, implementing a visual representation of your goals that enables you to assess progress at a glance. Visualizing your timeline cultivates a sense of accountability and helps ensure that you remain on track. Just as an archer assesses their standing at various points in a competition, regularly reviewing your upcoming tasks enhances awareness of your timeline.

Flexibility is key within any schedule. While structure offers a roadmap for productivity, the nature of coding often necessitates adaptability, as new challenges or unexpected issues can arise. Intentionally build buffer periods into your schedule to accommodate unforeseen circumstances, allowing for fluidity in your workflow. Embrace the idea of adjusting your focus based on priorities, recognizing that shifts may lead you to dive deeper into critical tasks or allocate more time for debugging.

Furthermore, scheduling time for learning and personal development can be immensely beneficial. Engaging in self-directed study, attending workshops, or exploring online tutorials fosters growth and keeps your skills current. Dedicate specific periods within your calendar for learning, treating them with the same importance as project deadlines. This commitment cultivates a mindset of continuous improvement, much like an archer dedicating time to refine their technique and expand their skill set.

Reflective practices are equally important in solidifying your scheduling efforts. At the end of each week or coding session, take time to evaluate how well your schedule has worked out. Ask yourself questions: Did you achieve your goals? Were there tasks you underestimated? Did you encounter personal distractions? This reflection allows for careful adjustments, ensuring that your schedule continues to serve your evolving needs as a coder.

Emphasize the significance of work-life balance within your scheduling approach. In pursuing coding excellence, it's essential to recognize that time spent outside of work is equally important for creativity and well-being. Integrate personal time, hobbies, and social activities into your schedule, ensuring that you maintain a holistic balance between work and life. Just as an archer learns to disconnect from pressures and relaxation techniques in preparation for competition, coders must acknowledge the importance of personal time in fostering creativity and resilience.

Lastly, consider sharing your schedule with colleagues or peers. Collaborating on schedules can enhance accountability and create an atmosphere of collective support. By engaging with others and discussing your goals, you create a network of encouragement and feedback that can lead to an enriched coding experience—much like a community of archers training together toward a shared vision.

In conclusion, scheduling is a fundamental aspect of coding that acts as a guiding framework for enhancing productivity, creativity, and work-life balance. By establishing a consistent routine, incorporating breaks, fostering adaptability, and integrating opportunities for personal growth, you can cultivate a meaningful coding schedule that nurtures your journey. Each careful choice reflects the principles of a Zen archer—focused, intentional, and responsive. Embrace scheduling as a powerful tool in your coding arsenal, ensuring that each session brings you closer to your goals while promoting both purpose and mindfulness.

7.3. Streamlining Tasks and Projects

Streamlining tasks and projects within the Emacs environment is integral to achieving a smooth, efficient coding workflow. Just as a Zen archer meticulously prepares their equipment and surroundings to enhance focus and precision, so too must coders construct a workflow that minimizes distractions and maximizes productivity. In this exploration, we will delve into various tools, techniques, and philosophies that can be harnessed within Emacs to streamline the management of tasks and projects.

At the core of an effective workflow is the clear definition of tasks and projects. Start by establishing a roadmap that outlines the major goals you aim to achieve. This roadmap should encompass not only your long-term objectives but also the smaller, actionable steps required to get there. Utilizing a visual tool such as a mind map can be incredibly beneficial, helping you to visualize the relationships between tasks, prioritize them, and manage your time effectively. Similar to an archer determining their trajectory, laying out your tasks provides clarity and direction, steering you toward your objectives with intention.

In Emacs, several packages can significantly aid in task management. The integration of `org-mode`, for instance, transforms Emacs into a powerful task management tool that fosters an organized flow of work. By creating structured outlines, checklists, and project timelines, you can better manage your coding responsibilities. Begin by defining tasks as headings within your org files, utilizing nested lists to represent subtasks, deadlines, and dependencies. The inherent flexibility of org-mode allows you to adapt your task list to your needs, much like an archer adjusting their aim based on wind conditions or distance.

Leveraging the capabilities of `org-agenda` can further enhance your organizational efforts. This powerful feature aggregates tasks across your org files into a consolidated view, presenting you with a snapshot of your commitments for the day, week, or month. By setting priorities and deadlines for your tasks, you cultivate a sense of urgency and importance that drives accountability. In this way, you can approach each coding session with a specific focus, channeling the mindset of preparing for a focused shot with clarity and intention.

Collaboration can complicate project management, but with Emacs, you have options to streamline teamwork. Version control integration —particularly utilizing `magit` for Git—ensures that all team members can interact with the project efficiently. Magit's intuitive interface promotes fluid communication of changes and task statuses, while also allowing for seamless navigation through branches and pull requests. Regular collaborative meetings, paired with the use of Emacs for real-time communication or paired programming sessions, fosters a culture of transparency and cohesion.

In addition to task management, incorporating time management into your workflow is essential. The Pomodoro Technique, already mentioned, can be effectively integrated into your task management system. Each coding session can be treated as a discrete task to be chunked into focused bursts, with the timer facilitating a structured work break. By evaluating your productivity post each "Pomodoro," you can adjust the pacing and scheduling of future sessions to align with your natural productivity rhythms—a method that cultivates a balance reminiscent of a Zen practice.

While tools and techniques play a significant role in streamlining tasks and projects, it is also important to regularly review your processes. Carve out time, perhaps on a weekly or monthly basis, to reflect on the efficiency of your workflow. Evaluate what methods and practices are serving you well and what areas require adjustment. Document this reflection to identify patterns or triggers that affect your productivity. Through this iterative process of evaluation and modification, your workflow evolves with you, allowing for continual refinement—a practice fundamental to both Zen and coding mastery.

Moreover, keeping the balance of form versus function in mind will aid your efficiency. Aim for a clean, readable codebase that aligns with your workflow. As you streamline your tasks, pay attention to the organization of your code itself. Ensuring that your functions are concise and your variables are clearly named reduces cognitive load, allowing you to direct your focus where it matters most.

Lastly, engaging with community-driven resources—such as blogs, forums, and tutorials—can expose you to innovative task management strategies that others have successfully employed. As an archer benefits from shared knowledge and techniques, so can you find inspiration and guidance within the coding community. Embrace the opportunity to learn from others, adopting practices that resonate with your approach while integrating them into your own workflow.

In conclusion, streamlining tasks and projects in Emacs is about cultivating an organized, intentional workflow that embodies the principles of clarity and focus. By establishing a roadmap, leveraging packages like org-mode, implementing time management techniques, collaborating effectively, and reflecting regularly on your practices, you create a responsive coding environment that allows for growth and efficacy. Just as a Zen archer hits their target with precision through rigorous practice, you too can create a streamlined workflow that empowers you to achieve your coding aspirations with ease and mindfulness. Embrace the journey, and let each task become an arrow shot toward your goals.

7.4. Enhancing Workflow with Plugins

Enhancing workflow with plugins is paramount in creating an efficient and tailored Emacs environment that aligns with your coding approach. Just as a Zen archer carefully selects tools that complement their skills and techniques, integrating the right plugins into Emacs can effectively elevate your productivity while nurturing a mindful workflow that promotes clarity and purpose.

To begin, consider the existing plugins within the Emacs ecosystem. These plugins extend the capabilities of Emacs beyond its core functionality, providing specialized tools to streamline various aspects of your coding process. Some popular Emacs plugins include:

1. Flycheck: Flycheck is a modern syntax checking extension that provides real-time feedback on your code as you type. It integrates with various programming languages and helps catch errors and warnings instantly. The immediacy of feedback allows you to address issues promptly and navigate your coding journey with confidence, much like an archer receiving immediate feedback on their shots.

2. Company Mode: This completion framework enhances your coding experience by providing on-the-fly code suggestions based on your current context. With Company Mode, you can expect intelligent auto-completions, significantly reducing the effort required to write code. This fluidity mirrors an archer's ability to seamlessly transition between shots, allowing you to maintain focus on your thought process rather than getting bogged down with syntax.

3. Magit: Magit is an exceptional Git interface for Emacs that offers an intuitive interface to interact with Git repositories seamlessly. It simplifies tasks such as staging, committing, and reviewing changes, allowing you to focus on code quality without being distracted by version control intricacies. Using Magit effectively transforms time-intensive version control processes into moments

of harmony, akin to an archer maintaining their flow despite the challenges of a competition.

4. Org Mode: While commonly used for task management and note-taking, Org Mode also serves as a powerful tool for managing coding projects. With its ability to organize tasks, track progress, and maintain notes, Org Mode creates a framework that encourages clarity and organization—essential qualities that resonate with effective coding practices. Utilizing Org Mode optimizes your workflow, ensuring you approach coding with intent, similar to an archer who plans their shot meticulously.

5. Projectile: For larger coding projects, Projectile enhances project management within Emacs. It allows you to quickly navigate through different files, manage project settings, and perform searches across your codebase. The ease of navigation through extensive projects reduces cognitive load, enabling you to remain engaged and focused on your coding tasks, much like an archer who navigates the range effortlessly.

6. Rainbow Delimiters: If you're working with nested structures, Rainbow Delimiters provides visual cues by color-coding parentheses and brackets. This plugin enhances readability, allowing you to track logical structures quickly without straining your focus, akin to the clear sight of a Zen archer.

As you integrate these plugins, remember that too many plugins can clutter your environment and diminish productivity. Mindfulness in your workflow is about crafting an environment that resonates with your style and fosters creativity. Take the time to assess the functionalities that align with your needs, focusing on plugins that enhance your workflow without creating unnecessary complexity. This tailoring reflects the essence of Zen—simplifying your environment while ensuring it serves a profound purpose.

With the right plugins in place, it's essential to revisit your workflow regularly—reflect on what works, what doesn't, and how you can further optimize your processes. This iterative evaluation ensures that your Emacs environment evolves alongside your coding journey, allowing for continual adaptation and improvement. Similar to an archer who refines their technique through ongoing practice, you should embrace change as a natural aspect of your coding experience.

Additionally, don't hesitate to explore the Emacs community to discover new plugins or strategies that resonate with your workflow. Engaging with fellow Emacs users can lead to insights, recommendations, and shared experiences that enhance your own understanding.

In conclusion, enhancing your workflow with plugins can profoundly transform your Emacs experience, allowing you to achieve greater efficiency and focus in your coding practice. Select plugins mindfully, ensuring they align with your goals and reflect the principles of simplicity and clarity embodied by Zen practice. As you integrate these tools into your environment, remain open to the possibilities they present and allow them to elevate your coding journey to new heights, much like the Zen archer poised to hit the bullseye with every shot. Embrace the journey of enhancement, and let each line of code resonate with intention, purpose, and precisely aimed precision.

7.5. Reviewing and Improving Your Workflow

As you reflect on your workflow, think of it as a bowstring being adjusted towards the target. Each aspect of your workflow represents a component that, when aligned correctly, allows you to release your ideas with precision and confidence. Just as the Zen archer constantly refines their stance, grip, and breathing to achieve accuracy, so too should you engage in the process of reviewing and improving your workflow.

Start by assessing the current state of your workflow. This involves taking a step back to examine how you approach coding tasks, project management, and time allocation. Consider the tools you use, the methodologies you embrace, and the patterns that either empower or hinder your productivity. Document your steps, frustrations, and points of joy to gain a comprehensive picture of your current practices.

To facilitate this evaluation, ask yourself specific questions. Are the tools you use meeting your needs? Are there features you wish to have at your fingertips that you currently lack? Reflect on pain points: areas where you feel stuck, overwhelmed, or inefficient. Like an archer analyzing their form after each round, identifying these aspects allows you to determine which elements of your workflow require adjustment.

Once you've established a baseline, begin to experiment with changes. This could involve introducing new plugins that enhance your Emacs environment, adopting novel coding practices, or implementing a new task management strategy. For example, if you find yourself hampered by distractions, consider using org-mode to create a structured list of tasks, breaking them into smaller, achievable components. Integrating the Pomodoro Technique can also serve to boost your focus by creating intervals of concentrated work, punctuated by short breaks.

Reevaluation is an ongoing practice. Allocate time periodically—perhaps weekly or bi-weekly—to reflect on the adjustments you've made. This cycle allows you to gather insights on what behaves well and what may need further refinement. Engage in a process similar to a Zen archer assessing their performance through focused practice. Embrace a growth mindset; this practice should not feel burdensome but rather be an enjoyable journey of continuous improvement.

Openness to feedback from peers can also enhance your workflow review. Engaging with colleagues provides fresh perspectives, allowing you to identify areas of your workflow that may not align with best practices. Just as an archer learns from observing fellow practitioners, you may glean insights and strategies that resonate with you. Create opportunities for collaborative reviews, both on code and workflow practices, to promote a supportive environment.

Additionally, remain mindful of your overall goals as you refine your workflow. What are your long-term objectives, and how does your current workflow help you achieve them? Aligning your improvements with your aspirations fosters a more meaningful sense of purpose in your practices. Devote time to reflecting on how each element of your workflow reflects your personal coding philosophy, a practice reminiscent of the deep introspection found in Zen.

Incorporating technological advancements is also essential to improving your workflow. Regularly explore new Emacs plugins, languages, and coding paradigms that could benefit your practice. Just as an archer strives to incorporate new insights into their technique —and perhaps upgrades their bow—staying current with evolving practices in coding can offer efficiencies and open new possibilities in your work.

Lastly, celebrate your progress through this process. As you implement changes and find improvements in your workflow, take time to acknowledge the achievements. Each minor milestone can bolster motivation and further energize your journey. Just as an archery competition culminates in recognition of the skill developed over time, so too should the journey through evolving your workflow provide satisfaction and inspiration.

In conclusion, the process of reviewing and improving your workflow is an essential endeavor that shapes your coding practice. By applying mindfulness, reflective evaluation, and openness to change, you align your workflow with your aspirations as a coder. Just as a Zen archer hits the bullseye through continuous refinement of technique, so too can you achieve clarity and precision in your coding journey by continually revising and enhancing your approach to work. Embrace this journey as its own target, set your sights forward, and collectively work towards mastery in your craft.

8. Zen and the Art of Coding Under Pressure

8.1. Keeping Calm in Code Crises

In the world of software development, encountering crises during coding is not just common; it's an inevitable reality. Whether it's debugging a complex issue right before a deadline, integration woes, or unexpected changes in project scope, navigating these moments can be intense and overwhelming. "Keeping Calm in Code Crises" emphasizes the significance of maintaining composure and mindfulness during these high-stress situations—transforming panic into focused action, much like a Zen archer adjusting their aim in the heat of competition.

To begin, the first step in managing code crises is to cultivate a mindset rooted in mindfulness and awareness. When panic begins to creep in, take a moment to pause and breathe. Deep breathing exercises can act as an immediate remedy to counteract the body's stress response. Inhale deeply through the nose, hold for a moment, and exhale slowly through the mouth. This simple act grounds you in the present moment, helping to regain control over racing thoughts. The clarity brought on by mindful breathing allows you to approach the coding crisis with a calm focus—a crucial state for effective problem-solving.

Next, it's important to acknowledge the emotional response that crises often provoke. Feelings of frustration, anxiety, or even despair can bubble to the surface when faced with a daunting coding issue. Rather than suppressing these feelings, adopt a mindful approach to recognize and accept them. Understand that these emotions are natural reactions, but they do not define your capabilities as a coder. Accepting these feelings allows you to create a supportive internal dialogue that encourages resilience and clarity. This aligns with the Zen practice of embracing and understanding one's emotions without judgment, turning internal chaos into strength.

Once you have established a state of calmness, engage in active problem-solving by breaking down the issue at hand. Instead of fixating on the crisis as an insurmountable obstacle, approach it as a series of smaller, manageable tasks. Ask questions: What specifically is the problem? What changes were made prior to the issue arising? Which areas of the code require investigation? By taking a step back and decompressing the problem, you bring structure to the chaos—much like an archer analyzing their shooting form in a focused assessment before taking aim.

Utilizing the debugging tools available in Emacs can significantly enhance your crisis management. Make use of the built-in edebug and debuggers for different languages. Set breakpoints strategically to stop execution where needed, enabling you to inspect variables and track down the source of errors. The key is to view bugs not merely as sources of frustration but as learning opportunities—each piece of feedback from your code can lead to greater understanding. This is akin to refining an archery technique through analyzing each shot, honing the skill for future performance.

Adopting a systematic approach to documentation during crises is another essential strategy. Keep detailed notes of changes made, errors encountered, and potential solutions explored. This practice serves two purposes: it provides a reference for future crises and creates an opportunity for reflective learning once the issue is resolved. Use comments within your code to address ambiguous sections or known issues, ensuring you leave behind helpful breadcrumbs that can guide you—or your future self—when similar situations arise.

Community engagement can also play a crucial role when navigating code crises. When facing tough challenges, don't hesitate to reach out to peers or mentors who can offer fresh perspectives. Discussing obstacles with others can provide insight and advice that may not have been considered. Similar to how archers consult coaches for feedback, sharing your coding difficulties fosters a collaborative environment of learning. Remember that you are not alone; the coding community is vast and supportive, offering camaraderie in times of struggle.

Additionally, practicing self-compassion is vital in the face of coding crises. Remind yourself that mistakes are inherent to the learning process. Rather than dwelling on self-criticism, offer yourself the same kindness you would extend to a colleague facing the same challenges. Accepting imperfection contributes to a resilient mindset, allowing you to embrace crises as part of the coding journey. Acknowledge that every coder has failed and struggled at moments. These experiences shape growth and mastery over time.

Once the crisis is resolved, take a moment to reflect on what transpired. Consider what strategies worked well and which areas could benefit from refinement in similar future situations. Constructively review your responses to the crisis and pull valuable lessons that will inform your approach going forward. This reflection solidifies growth and resilience, much like how an archer analyzes performance statistics to refine future training.

In summary, "Keeping Calm in Code Crises" is an invitation to foster mindfulness and resilience in the face of challenges. Through practices such as deep breathing, acknowledging emotions, breaking down problems, utilizing debugging tools, documenting effectively, seeking support, and practicing self-compassion, you can transform code crises into opportunities for growth and learning. Embracing the process allows you to navigate these turbulent moments with the calm assurance of a Zen archer, ultimately empowering you to hit the coding bullseye with confidence and clarity.

8.2. From Pressure to Progress

In the journey of coding, it is natural to encounter periods of intense pressure, whether due to looming project deadlines, unexpected bugs that demand immediate attention, or the weight of high expectations from team members and stakeholders. However, learning to transform pressure into progress is a crucial skill that can turn a seemingly overwhelming situation into a productive experience. This approach not only reflects the essence of a Zen mindset but also aligns with effective coding strategies that emphasize clarity, focus, and resilience.

The foundation of transitioning from pressure to progress lies in acknowledging the emotional responses that arise when faced with pressure. When deadlines approach or urgent issues arise, it is common to experience anxiety or stress. In these moments, it is essential to practice mindfulness—an integral component of Zen philosophy. Being present with your feelings can help you recognize and address them without judgment. Engage in a few deep breaths, allowing yourself to reconnect with the task at hand and foster a sense of calm amidst the chaos. This grounding technique creates space for clear thinking and focused problem-solving, essential elements when facing urgent coding challenges.

Once mindful, the next step towards progress involves breaking down the tasks at hand into manageable components. Rather than becoming overwhelmed by the entirety of the work, identify specific actions that can be tackled one at a time. For example, if a major feature must be completed by the end of the week, segment the work into discrete parts—design the interface, implement functions, and write tests. By viewing the project through these smaller lenses, you can prioritize tasks based on urgency and importance, steering your focus towards one achievable goal at a time, much like an archer who draws their attention to each shot rather than getting distracted by the overall score.

Time management extends this fragmenting approach beyond mere task breakdowns. Utilize techniques such as the Pomodoro Technique, where you dedicate focused time blocks to writing code followed by short, restorative breaks. This method reinforces discipline and helps manage time efficiently. It encourages you to maintain focus without burning out, allowing the mind to reset between intervals—similar to an archer who takes a moment before each shot to align their focus. Within those focused intervals, put your energy into quality work, ensuring each keystroke reflects intention and thoughtfulness, even under tight pressure.

Furthermore, leverage the tools at your disposal. Embrace Emacs's robust features—such as its powerful editing commands, built-in terminal, and version control integrations—to ease your workload and minimize fuss. When faced with pressure, relying on the right tools can significantly boost your efficiency and effectiveness. For example, use `magit` to seamlessly manage Git operations without leaving your coding flow, and employ `company-mode` for intelligent code completion that reduces syntactical errors and improves productivity. Allow these tools to act as extensions of your abilities, enabling you to maintain your focus and clarity amidst urgent timelines.

When you do encounter mistakes or bugs amidst the pressure, practice the Zen principles of patience and humility. Recognize that each error presents an opportunity for growth and learning. Rather than lashing out or growing frustrated, treat each bug as a puzzle to be solved. This perspective fosters resilience and a healthier emotional response to coding challenges, helping you navigate through crisis points constructively. Document these challenges, recording not only the solutions but also the lessons learned. This practice acts as a resource for future reference, creating a repository of knowledge that can serve you in times of similarity.

Support from colleagues and peers is another asset during high-pressure moments. When feeling overwhelmed, don't hesitate to reach out for help or feedback. Collaborative problem-solving is a powerful strategy that can relieve stress and lead to innovative solutions. Much like an archer who might train with a coach to refine their skills, engaging with others in the coding community promotes learning and collective growth. Embrace the diversity of perspectives that others can offer; working as a team lightens the load and often leads to breakthroughs.

Lastly, upon emerging from periods of pressure, devote time to reflection. Assess what worked, what didn't, and how you can further streamline your approach for future pressures. Drawing from your experiences strengthens your coding journey and illuminates areas for continuous improvement moving forward. Incorporate lessons learned into your coding philosophy, ensuring each challenge enhances your overall skill set—much like an archer improving their technique with each practice session.

In conclusion, mastering the art of transforming pressure into progress requires a cohesive blend of mindfulness, organization, effective use of tools, collaboration, and self-reflection. By incorporating these practices into your coding routine, you can navigate challenges with a Zen-like composure, turning potential crises into opportunities for growth. Embrace the journey with clarity and purpose, and you'll consistently hit your coding targets, emerging from pressure not as defeated, but as a stronger, more capable coder.

8.3. Effective Communication Under Stress

Effective communication under stress is a vital skill for any professional coder, especially in the fast-paced and often high-pressure environments encountered in software development. In the throes of a coding crisis—be it a looming deadline, a critical bug, or miscommunication with teammates—the ability to articulate thoughts clearly, remain composed, and foster open dialogue can significantly impact project success and team cohesion. This subchapter will explore practical strategies to maintain effective communication during times of stress, drawing upon the principles of Zen to cultivate a mindful approach that enhances understanding and collaboration.

At the core of effective communication is the necessity to stay composed and focused. Stress can easily cloud judgment and lead to emotional reactions that hinder clear expression. Just as a Zen archer must find their center before releasing an arrow, you must take a moment to ground yourself before engaging in critical conversations. Begin by acknowledging the stressors at play; recognize your feelings without becoming immersed in them. Techniques such as mindful breathing can help eliminate immediate anxiety. Inhale deeply, hold for a moment, and exhale slowly—this practice calms the nervous system and allows you to engage with a sense of clarity.

Once grounded, consider the message you wish to convey. Being clear about your thoughts is paramount, especially in high-pressure scenarios. Structure your communication to ensure it is concise and to the point. Avoid jargon or technical language that may not be understood by all parties involved. If a critical bug emerged and you must communicate it to your team, outline the main points: what the issue is, its potential impact, the urgency of the situation, and any preliminary solutions or actions taken. Following this clarity, ensure that your tone remains calm and steady—this fosters an environment of collective problem-solving rather than introducing panic or uncertainty.

Effective listening is equally crucial in enhancing communication. During stressful moments, it becomes easy to interrupt or overlook what others are saying. However, fostering an atmosphere of active listening is essential for successful collaboration. When a colleague raises concerns or suggests solutions, provide them with your undivided attention. Acknowledge their input by summarizing what they've expressed before offering your perspective. This practice not only demonstrates respect but also enhances an environment of support—a mutual understanding that brings the team closer together in pursuit of a common goal.

In coding environments, misunderstandings can escalate into larger issues if not addressed promptly. Encourage a culture of open feedback, where team members feel comfortable voicing concerns or seeking clarification. When initiating a dialogue, frame your approach with curiosity rather than defensiveness. For instance, if receiving feedback on one's code, instead of reacting with a defensive stance, ask questions that seek to unpack their perspective: "Can you explain why you believe this approach may be problematic?" This creates a collaborative atmosphere that values constructive engagement.

Furthermore, harness the power of technology to streamline communication, especially when working remotely or with distributed teams. Use chat applications like Slack or other organizational tools to create dedicated channels for discussions related to specific projects or challenges. This approach ensures that conversations remain organized, allowing for seamless reference and reducing the likelihood of miscommunication. Documenting key decisions, discussions, and feedback can also serve as a point of truth, providing clarity and preventing misunderstandings as projects evolve.

As stress levels rise, tensions may cloud rational discourse. In such cases, it may be beneficial to take strategic breaks to reset the conversation. Stepping away for a short duration can foster psychological distance, allowing individuals to regroup before re-engaging in discussions. Establishing this practice within a team culture not only enhances communication but also bolsters emotional resilience, reducing the impact of stress on interpersonal dynamics.

Finally, introducing consistent touchpoints for team communication can help maintain alignment and cohesion. Regular stand-up meetings, progress check-ins, and retrospectives provide opportunities to connect and evaluate the health of the project. These sessions facilitate open communication concerning expectations, challenges, and insights, allowing the team to collectively navigate stressors while remaining committed to shared objectives.

In conclusion, effective communication under stress is a critical competency that can significantly shape the trajectory of coding projects. By cultivating a mindful approach grounded in clarity, active listening, open feedback, technology utilization, strategic breaks, and consistent touchpoints, you can enhance team collaboration and navigate crises effectively. Embracing Zen principles in your communication practices fosters an atmosphere of understanding and respect, while empowering you to channel the focused intention of a Zen archer —ensuring that every conversation helps advance the collective aim towards project success.

8.4. Mindful Time Management

Effective time management is an essential skill for coders, as it allows for the allocation of focused attention to various tasks while maintaining a balance between productivity and personal well-being. Within the Emacs environment, mindful time management takes on a unique flavor, allowing you to harness the powerful features of Emacs while embodying the principles of Zen, which encourages awareness, presence, and intentionality. This section will explore strategies for developing a mindful approach to time management, enabling you to manage your coding sessions with clarity and purpose.

To begin, setting clear goals for each coding session is vital. When you approach your work with intentionality, you can differentiate between tasks that require deep concentration and those that can be accomplished with less focus. Take a moment to define your objectives before diving into your coding work—ask yourself what you hope to achieve in that session and what success will look like. This sets the stage for a productive time allocation that mirrors the Zen practice of setting clear intentions before embarking on a task.

Next, integrate the Pomodoro Technique into your coding practice. This structured approach, involving focused work intervals followed by short breaks, cultivates productive flow while allowing for moments of rejuvenation. An example would be working in 25-minute increments, followed by a 5-minute break to stretch or breathe deeply. After every four cycles, consider taking a longer break—15-30 minutes. This technique reflects the Zen principle of balance between focused effort and necessary rest, allowing your mind to recharge and maintain clarity during intense coding sessions.

As you manage your coding time, be mindful of the distractions that may surround you. In the fast-paced world of technology, notifications, emails, and other interruptions can easily disrupt your focus. Minimizing distractions involves creating a conducive environment where you can immerse yourself fully in your coding tasks. Ensure that your workspace is tidy, eliminate unnecessary tabs or applications running on your computer, and establish boundaries around your time, such as using "Do Not Disturb" settings. This helps create a respectful space for your concentration, much like the disciplined setup an archer maintains during practice.

Fostering a habit of self-reflection is also critical for developing mindful time management skills. At the end of each coding session, take a few moments to evaluate how well you managed your time. Did you stick to your goals? Were there tasks that took longer than expected? Reflecting on these questions allows you to adapt your future coding sessions, honing your time management strategies and enhancing your overall productivity. This ongoing practice of reflection mirrors the way a Zen archer may analyze their performance to identify areas for improvement.

Another aspect of mindful time management is recognizing your energy levels throughout the day. Different tasks require varying degrees of cognitive effort, and being aware of when you feel most focused can significantly impact your productivity. Schedule challenging tasks during your peak energy times, whether that's in the morning, midday, or evening. By aligning complex coding tasks with your natural rhythm, you can engage in a more efficient and effective workflow, akin to an archer timing their shots based on conditions and focus.

Consider blocking time for specific types of tasks using your Emacs environment tools such as `org-agenda`. The integration of `org-mode` allows you to visualize your tasks and appointments, providing a clear snapshot of your commitments. By scheduling focused blocks for coding, meetings, and breaks, you empower yourself to manage your time more effectively. This visual representation cultivates a sense of direction and enhances accountability, enabling you to approach your workflow with clarity and intention.

Flexibility is another cornerstone of mindful time management. Despite careful planning, setbacks and new tasks are inevitable in coding. When faced with unexpected challenges or interruptions, strive to embrace adaptability rather than frustration. Allow yourself the grace to shift your schedule as needed, recognizing that it's a fluid process. This aligns with Zen principles, which promote acceptance and a positive response to changing circumstances.

Finally, integrate moments of gratitude and appreciation into your time management practice. Acknowledging the accomplishments made during your coding sessions—whether large or small—reinforces motivation and positivity. Celebrate your progress, recognizing that each line of code written brings you closer to your overarching goals. This practice enhances your awareness of the journey and encourages a sense of fulfillment in your work, enriching both your personal and professional coding experience.

In conclusion, mindful time management in the context of coding encompasses clear goal-setting, the application of techniques like the Pomodoro Technique, minimization of distractions, self-reflection, awareness of energy levels, strategic use of tools, and the cultivation of adaptability and gratitude. By implementing these strategies, you can navigate your coding responsibilities with clarity, focus, and purpose, ultimately fostering a harmonious relationship with your work that embodies the principles of Zen. As you master the art of mindful time management, you will hit your targets with every coding session, leading to a fulfilling and enriching coding journey.

8.5. The Zen of Post-Deadline Reflection

In the realm of coding, the moments that follow the completion of a project — especially after a tight deadline — can be reflective, revealing, and crucial for personal and professional growth. As Zen practitioners emphasize the importance of reflection, the archer retrieves their arrows after the shot, takes a deep breath, and assesses their performance. Post-deadline reflection in coding embodies this practice, offering a structured way to analyze successes and challenges, celebrate achievements, and identify areas for continued growth.

Firstly, it is essential to earmark a specific time for reflection once the rush of a project has subsided. Many developers fall into the trap of immediately jumping into the next task and neglecting the vital act of reviewing their work. Just as the Zen archer dedicates moments to assess each shot's outcome, coders should allow themselves that same grace. Set aside a period, perhaps on a Friday or at the end of a sprint, to review the completed project holistically, contemplating both the technical outcomes and the emotional journey.

Begin this reflective practice by reviewing your initial goals and objectives for the project. What were the expected deliverables, and how did they align with your actual outcomes? Engage in self-inquiry: Did you hit the intended coding targets, and if not, what factors contributed to those discrepancies? This step allows for a candid evaluation, much like an archer inspecting their bow and arrows post-practice to discern what could be improved.

Celebrate successes, big and small, during your reflection. What accomplishments are you proud of? Perhaps you implemented a particularly complex feature, resolved stubborn bugs that seemed insurmountable, or streamlined your coding process with a new Emacs workflow. Eliciting a sense of gratitude and acknowledgment fosters a positive mindset, reinforcing the enjoyment of coding — key principles found in both Zen and archer training. Document these achievements in a way that resonates with you, as this serves as a motivational reminder for future projects.

In tandem with celebrating successes, scrutinize areas that fell short during the project. Acknowledge moments where you may have rushed through tasks or where features did not meet expectations. What could be done differently? Perhaps time management strategies could be improved, or the importance of pre-implementation testing highlighted more profoundly. This honest self-assessment parallels the practice of a Zen archer determining where adjustments are needed, ultimately strengthening future performances by developing a clearer understanding of past challenges.

Solicit feedback from peers or mentors who were involved in the project. Viewing the completed work through the eyes of others can reveal insights you might not have considered. Inviting constructive criticism fosters collaborative learning and reinforces the interconnectedness often emphasized in Zen thinking. Provide your team with the opportunity to speak candidly about the project's best practices and challenges, stimulating discussion and growth.

As you gather reflections from both personal introspection and peer feedback, create a plan for actionable improvements in future coding endeavors. It could be adopting new methodologies, utilizing estimation tools to improve project timelines, or enhancing your testing framework to catch issues earlier in the process. This structured action plan imbues your reflections with purpose and direction, nurturing a commitment to continuous improvement.

Zen philosophy also encourages gratitude for the journey itself. Appreciate the struggles and victories alike, recognizing that they contribute to your evolving mastery as a coder. Treat each project as investment in your skills rather than as finite endeavors, and embrace the wisdom gained from both successes and failures. This mindset shift turns your coding journey into an enriching experience — mentally, emotionally, and technically.

Also, consider documenting your reflections in a journal, blog, or even in your Emacs setup with org-mode. Creating a log of insights, accomplishments, and proposed changes fosters a personalized knowledge repository. Additionally, it will serve you in the long run; revisiting past reflections can be illuminating for future projects when faced with similar challenges.

In summary, the practice of post-deadline reflection transcends mere evaluation of a completed project. It represents a critical aspect of personal and professional growth in coding. By honoring the process through which you have just gone, celebrating successes, analyzing challenges, and identifying areas for improvement, you cultivate a mindful approach that integrates the essence of Zen into your coding philosophy. Embrace the opportunity to learn, grow, and reflect, fostering an enriching coding journey ahead, ensuring that every project taken is an arrow well-aligned with your unique trajectory toward mastery.

9. Integrating Emacs into the Professional Environment

9.1. Deploying Emacs in Team Projects

Deploying Emacs in team projects involves a careful balance between facilitating individual productivity and fostering effective collaboration among team members. This section focuses on the strategies and practices that can help integrate Emacs into the larger team environment, maximizing its benefits while ensuring compatibility with team dynamics and tools.

To begin with, it's critical to establish a common ground in how Emacs is used across team members. This integration process may begin with setting up a default Emacs configuration that includes shared packages and practices. Identifying core plugins that promote functionality and streamline processes—such as `magit` for Git integration, `projectile` for project management, and `flycheck` for real-time syntax checking—can help create a standardized working environment. By sharing your `init.el` or configuration files across the team, members benefit from a cohesive Emacs experience that reduces friction during collaborative coding sessions.

Moreover, aligning on coding standards is essential when deploying Emacs for team projects. Implementing style guides and common practices ensures that the codebase remains consistent and maintainable. Emacs, with its flexible configuration options, allows you to easily bind specific coding styles and linters to the major modes you're using. For instance, integrating `lsp-mode` can provide IDE-like features including auto-completion, code navigation, and error reporting across multiple programming languages. Establishing these guidelines from the onset not only fosters a shared understanding among team members but also helps maintain clarity and intention in your coding practices.

Communication within the team is key, especially when working with Emacs as your primary editor. Regularly scheduled check-ins or collaborative sessions provide clear channels for sharing updates and resolving challenges. Emphasizing an open-door policy for discussing Emacs usage can help identify pain points or areas where additional training or resources might be necessary. Encouraging team members to share tips, tricks, or customizations fosters an environment of growth and support—contributing to overall productivity and morale.

Integrating version control tools like Git into your Emacs workflow also plays a significant role in deploying Emacs within team projects. Using `magit` for version control not only simplifies Git operations but also enhances collaboration by allowing team members to easily review each other's contributions. Establishing a centralized Git repository encourages practices such as pull requests, enabling code review discussions directly in the Emacs environment. This approach not only promotes efficient code review processes but also allows for immediate context around proposed changes, allowing team members to engage collaboratively with the existing codebase.

In addition to standardizing practices and tools, it's crucial to create a culture of collective ownership and responsibility. Encourage developers to take part in all aspects of the project—not just coding—but also documentation, testing, and deployment. Emphasizing shared accountability ensures that all team members remain engaged and committed to the success of the project. Just like Zen archers training collaboratively, sharing information and insights strengthens the team's bond and enhances performance.

It's also wise to incorporate regular retrospectives to assess how well Emacs is serving the team's needs. These retrospectives can focus not only on the technical aspects of Emacs but also on team dynamics and communication. Continuous improvement should be celebrated, embracing successes while remaining open to addressing challenges. This reflective practice embodies the Zen philosophy of growth through introspection and encourages ongoing adaptations to the Emacs deployment as the project evolves.

Lastly, educating team members about Emacs can facilitate a smoother deployment. Offering training sessions or workshops can introduce less experienced users to the powerful features and work-flows available within Emacs, helping them integrate quickly and confidently. As team members become more comfortable with the environment, they can leverage Emacs's extensibility and flexibility to streamline their individual coding practices.

In conclusion, deploying Emacs in team projects involves creating a cohesive and supportive environment that maximizes individual productivity while fostering collaboration. Establishing shared configurations, aligning on coding standards, integrating version control, promoting open communication, encouraging collective ownership, incorporating regular retrospectives, and facilitating training contribute to an effective Emacs deployment across the team. By carefully weaving these elements together, teams can achieve enhanced productivity and a unified approach, ultimately leading to successful project outcomes with a Zen-like focus on mastery and mindfulness in coding.

9.2. Collaborative Coding in Emacs

Collaborative coding in Emacs is an empowering way to foster teamwork and enhance communication among coders. In an era where development often occurs in distributed settings, having tools and practices that enable real-time collaboration becomes paramount. Emacs, with its unique extensibility and customization capabilities, offers various approaches to collaborative coding that can enhance team dynamics and improve project outcomes.

The cornerstone of effective collaboration begins with choosing the right tools to facilitate shared coding efforts. Emacs can integrate seamlessly with various version control systems, particularly Git, using packages such as Magit. Magit transforms how teams manage version control, offering visual interfaces and commands that simplify tasks like staging changes, reviewing diffs, and committing code. By adopting Magit for collaborative work, team members can engage with the codebase dynamically, making it easy to discuss changes and review contributions without the friction commonly associated with command-line Git operations.

In addition to version control, setting up a shared Emacs configuration can significantly enhance the collaborative experience. By creating a baseline setup that includes commonly used plugins, configurations, and themes, teams can ensure that everyone is on the same page when coding. Shared configurations can be stored in a centralized repository accessible by all team members. This approach ensures consistency in coding practices and promotes camaraderie, akin to a group of archers training together under a shared philosophy and aiming toward common targets.

For real-time collaboration, integrating Emacs with tools like Teletype for Atom or using packages such as `emacs-mu4e` alongside `org-mode` for shared notes can foster synchronous coding sessions. Though Elisp does not typically provide built-in real-time collaborative features, the Emacs community continually evolves, contributing libraries and plugins that facilitate collaborative coding endeavors. By experimenting with these tools during pair programming sessions or hackathons, teams can bridge the geographical divide and work together cohesively.

Effective communication is paramount when engaging in collaborative coding. Establishing communication channels, such as dedicated chat rooms via Slack or Discord, enables team members to discuss code implementations, share troubleshooting strategies, and brainstorm ideas in real time. These discussions can be supplemented with regular video check-ins to enhance personal connections within the team, reinforcing bonds that positively impact collaboration.

Within coding sessions, fostering a growth mindset is crucial. Encourage team members to embrace mistakes as learning opportunities rather than perceived failures. This environment cultivates psychological safety, allowing everyone to share ideas freely without fear of blame. Just as an archer analyzes their shot to identify areas for improvement, encourage team members to engage in open discussions about the challenges they encounter, highlighting the insights gained in the process.

To maximize the benefits of collaborative coding, documenting processes, decisions, and code snippets becomes essential. Utilize `org-mode` to create shared documentation that records decisions made during coding sessions, definitions of functions, or the rationale behind specific implementations. This habit not only serves as a reference for current project members, but also becomes an invaluable resource for future teams who may maintain or enhance the existing codebase.

Incorporating pair programming sessions can further enhance collaborative efforts. This practice involves two developers working together on the same code, with one taking the role of the driver (the one typing) and the other as the observer (the one reviewing). This real-time feedback loop creates an effective learning environment where code quality improves, and the team benefits from shared knowledge. Much like an archery duo practicing together to improve their accuracy, pair programming can build trust and foster collaboration.

Additionally, team retrospectives are invaluable in understanding the successes and areas for improvement within collaborative efforts. Set aside designated times post-project to reflect on the team's performance as a unit. Discuss what worked well during the coding process, the dynamics of collaboration, as well as challenges faced. This practice strengthens team cohesion and enhances future collaboration— paving the way for increased efficiency and productivity in upcoming projects.

In conclusion, collaborative coding in Emacs offers teams the chance to enhance productivity, communication, and cohesion through shared practices, effective tools, and open discourse. By implementing techniques such as using Magit for version control, establishing a common Emacs configuration, encouraging pair programming, and fostering a growth-oriented culture, teams can achieve impressive outcomes. Embrace the collaborative spirit, much like Zen archers training together, and empower each team member to contribute towards hitting the coding targets with clarity and purpose.

9.3. Emacs for Remote Work

In an increasingly remote world, the ability to seamlessly integrate technology and maintain productivity outside of traditional office settings has never been more essential. Emacs serves as a powerful tool for remote work, enabling coders to create and sustain efficient work environments—from anywhere. By employing the combination of Emacs's flexibility, extensibility, and commitment to mindful practices, remote workers can cultivate a workspace that promotes clarity, focus, and collaboration.

To successfully utilize Emacs in a remote work setting, begin with setting up a personalized Emacs configuration. This involves tailoring your `init.el` file to include essential packages that enhance productivity. Key add-ons might include `org-mode` for task management, `magit` for version control, and `company-mode` for code completion. Each of these packages contributes to creating a smooth workflow, helping you maintain focus on coding tasks without distractions. When moving from a traditional office environment to remote work, transitioning to Emacs's capabilities can make the experience more seamless and effective.

A stable internet connection is vital for remote work, with access to reliable communication tools such as Slack, Zoom, or Discord further enhancing collaboration with team members. Emacs facilitates this integration through various packages that support real-time editing, such as `emacs-live` or `Teletype`. These tools allow developers to work together on the same files in real-time, reminiscent of the collaborative spirit seen in coding huddles or workshops. By enabling live editing, you can promote agile workflows, ensuring connectivity even in remote setups.

Another advantage of using Emacs for remote work lies in its inherent customization capabilities. As remote teams often communicate across multiple time zones and vary in working styles, having a flexible environment tailored to individual preferences is essential. Embrace the practice of defining your coding preferences, workflows, themes, and keybindings in your Emacs configuration to ensure maximum comfort and efficiency in your remote coding experience. This custom environment allows you to maintain clarity and mindfulness as you immerse yourself in your work, regardless of physical location.

In addition, make use of Emacs's robust version control capabilities through Git integration. Collaborating on coding projects while working remotely necessitates efficient management of version control. Using `magit` simplifies Git operations directly from Emacs, enabling you to track changes, navigate branches, and resolve conflicts without leaving the coding environment. This streamlined experience minimizes disruptions and enhances focus, ensuring that you remain engaged in your work.

Organizing your tasks can also be effectively managed with Emacs, particularly using `org-mode`. Create structured to-do lists, deadlines, and project timelines within your Emacs setup. This practice resembles the disciplined approach of a Zen archer who maps out their training sessions. By outlining your objectives and preferred methods of execution, you pave the way for productive coding sessions. Additionally, using `org-agenda` allows you to visualize your tasks, promoting a clear understanding of priorities and deadlines amid remote work challenges.

Creating moments for mindful breaks during your work sessions is crucial for sustaining productivity while working remotely. Practicing scheduled breaks using techniques such as the Pomodoro Technique helps combat mental fatigue and promotes rejuvenation. Pausing to practice breathing exercises or simply stepping away from your workspace can restore clarity and focus, facilitating a more fruitful remote coding experience.

Regular communication among remote team members is essential for project success. Establish daily or weekly check-ins to discuss progress, obstacles, and insights. Embrace the principles of open dialogue, encouraging team members to share feedback and request assistance when needed. This culture of collaboration nurtures collective growth, connecting remote workers through the shared goal of coding excellence—much like a team of archers improving their skills through practice and support.

Lastly, integrate a reflective practice at the end of coding sessions or project milestones. Spend time assessing what worked well, what mid-term adaptations are necessary, and how to enhance the work-flow for future coding endeavors. Document this reflection to allow for continual growth—a practice that mirrors Zen teaching in the pursuit of understanding oneself and improving one's skills.

In summary, deploying Emacs in remote work environments offers unparalleled possibilities for maintaining productivity, collaboration, and mindfulness. With a customized setup, robust version control, effective task management, and a commitment to reflection, remote workers can create an effective coding experience that transcends physical boundaries. Embrace the adaptability of Emacs and the principles of Zen as you navigate the remote work landscape, ensuring your coding practices are not only efficient but also bring fulfillment and clarity to the journey ahead.

9.4. Interviewing with Emacs Skills

In today's rapidly evolving tech landscape, the ability to articulate and showcase your skills in interviews is vital for securing opportunities and fostering professional growth. For coders proficient in Emacs, demonstrating these skills during an interview requires a balance of technical capability and an understanding of how Emacs can enhance productivity and quality in coding practices. This subchapter explores strategies and practical tips for effectively presenting your Emacs skills during coding interviews, ensuring that you leave a lasting impression.

Begin by preparing a solid foundation of your Emacs knowledge. This entails having a deep understanding of both the fundamental and advanced functionalities of Emacs, including essential commands, package management, customization techniques, and workflow enhancements. Be ready to discuss your experience with popular Emacs packages that elevate your coding process, such as `magit` for Git integration, `flycheck` for on-the-fly syntax checking, and `org-mode` for task management. Being able to explain how these tools have contributed to your coding efficiency and quality will demonstrate your competency and adaptability as a coder.

A practical way to convey your Emacs experience is to prepare to discuss real-life coding scenarios where Emacs has been instrumental in your workflow. Illustrate specific challenges you've encountered and how you leveraged Emacs features or packages to overcome those hurdles. For instance, consider sharing an experience where you used `edebug` to identify and solve a particularly stubborn bug, detailing how the debugging process was streamlined by Emacs's built-in commands. Sharing these stories provides concrete evidence of your technical skills while simultaneously showcasing your problem-solving approach and capacity to learn from experiences.

When participating in technical interviews, be prepared for live coding exercises, where you may be asked to solve coding challenges on a shared platform or in an online code editor. In such scenarios, setting up Emacs in advance is crucial. Familiarize yourself with features that facilitate efficient coding, like code completion and navigation commands. Practice coding with real-time feedback from tools within Emacs. Communicate your thought process during the coding exercise, discussing your approach to solving the problem and utilizing Emacs features as you go along. This transparency not only highlights your technical prowess but also demonstrates your ability to think critically and communicate effectively under pressure.

As you prepare to discuss your skills, consider the Zen principles of mindfulness and reflection. Mindfulness emphasizes a focused, aware presence in your coding journey. During interviews, embody this principle by maintaining focus on the questions asked and responding thoughtfully and intentionally. Show an understanding of the nuances of coding and Emacs practices without rushing, modeling the patience inherent in effective coding. If you encounter challenging questions or situations during the interview, approach them calmly and take a moment to process your thoughts before responding.

Another key aspect of interviewing with Emacs skills is your ability to communicate code reviews and collaborative practices. Be prepared to share your experience working within a team, emphasizing how you leveraged Emacs to facilitate collaboration—whether through version control systems like Git or through shared documentations using org-mode. Discuss your philosophy on how effective collaboration enhances coding quality and your willingness to adapt your coding practices to meet team standards. This inherently demonstrates your ability as a collaborative coder while highlighting the strengths that come from using Emacs in a team setting.

During interviews, always be receptive to questions about your learning processes and adaptability. Be prepared to discuss how you keep your skills current and how you approach adopting new technologies. Since technology and best practices continually evolve, demonstrating a commitment to lifelong learning mirrors the Zen principle of continuous growth. Highlight how Emacs facilitates this journey for you by offering a customizable environment where iteration and experimentation are valued. Emphasizing this adaptability can resonate positively with hiring managers looking for candidates who are proactive and forward-thinking.

In conclusion, interviewing with Emacs skills requires not just an understanding of the tool itself but also the ability to communicate how it enhances coding practices, fosters collaboration, and embodies mindfulness in problem-solving. Preparing well, sharing real-world experiences, demonstrating a growth mindset, and embracing the principles of Zen in coding will help set you apart during interviews, ensuring that you leave an impression of competence and a passionate commitment to your craft. Embrace the journey with confidence, and let your Emacs mastery shine brightly in your professional endeavors.

9.5. Professional Growth with Emacs Mastery

Professional growth with Emacs mastery is a journey that weaves together technical skills with personal development, resulting in a holistic approach to coding. Embracing Emacs as your primary tool not only enhances your programming capabilities but also fosters disciplined practices that can accelerate your career growth. In this exploration, we'll delve deep into how mastering Emacs can serve as a catalyst for professional advancement and open the door to new opportunities, ultimately drawing inspiration from the principles of Zen.

First and foremost, becoming proficient in Emacs is akin to acquiring a specialized skill set that distinguishes you from other developers. As you invest time in mastering Emacs, you cultivate a unique edge that can be highlighted during interviews or performance reviews. The depth of customization available in Emacs allows you to tailor your environment to your personal workflow, paving the way for efficiency and clarity. Being able to articulate how Emacs has improved your coding practices offers a clear demonstration of your commitment to excellence and continuous improvement—qualities highly valued in any professional setting.

Moreover, Emacs's extensibility serves as a powerful springboard for deepening your understanding of programming, coding best practices, and even software development methodologies. Plugins like `magit` and `projectile` not only simplify your workflow but also expose you to the intricacies of version control and project management. By becoming adept in these areas, you position yourself as a valuable team member, ready to tackle challenges that intersect with collaboration and coding practices. This adaptability enhances your professional profile and enables you to contribute meaningfully to team projects.

Another vital aspect of professional growth involves networking and community engagement. Emacs is supported by a vibrant community of developers who are passionate about sharing knowledge and experiences. Participating in forums, contributing to discussions, or even writing about your own Emacs setup can significantly enhance your visibility in the tech community. As you become a part of this ecosystem, you may discover new opportunities, collaborations, or mentorships—all of which can accelerate your career trajectory. The connections formed within the community reflect the Zen principle of interconnectedness, where the sharing of expertise fosters collective growth.

In a fast-paced industry, staying curious and committed to lifelong learning is crucial for professional advancement. Emacs serves as a versatile framework for experimentation, enabling you to explore new coding paradigms, languages, and frameworks. The beauty of Emacs lies in its capacity to adapt to your evolving skill set, allowing for an environment where you can seamlessly integrate new knowledge and techniques. This adaptability can inspire innovation, presenting unique problem-solving approaches that make you stand out as a developer.

As you gain mastery over Emacs, remember to set clear goals for your professional growth. Just as an archer defines their objectives based on targets, you must take the time to evaluate where you would like to see yourself in your career. These goals may include mastering new programming languages, contributing to open-source projects, or honing soft skills critical for leadership. By defining these targets and employing Emacs as a tool to achieve them, you create a strategic pathway to your desired career trajectory.

Furthermore, mentoring others can solidify your knowledge and enhance your stature within the community. As you grow more confident in your Emacs skills, consider sharing your insights with newcomers, hosting workshops, or providing guidance on coding practices. Teaching not only reinforces your expertise but also underscores the Zen principle of compassion—devoting time to support others on their respective journeys. The act of mentoring nurtures an inclusive culture and fosters collaboration, elevating both your professional profile and the experiences of those around you.

As you navigate your professional growth, also embrace the importance of reflection. Engage in regular self-assessment to understand your strengths, weaknesses, and progress. Integrate this reflective practice into your workflow by documenting experiences, challenges, and successes along your journey. This habit mirrors the disciplined training regimen of a Zen archer, ensuring that every experience cultivated through Emacs translates into growth and mastery over time.

In conclusion, professional growth with Emacs mastery is a transformative journey that encompasses technical skills, community engagement, lifelong learning, and self-reflection. By embracing the flexibility and power of Emacs while integrating the philosophies of Zen, you position yourself for meaningful advancement and opportunities in your coding career. As you continue to cultivate your skills, remember that you are not just aiming to be a proficient coder; you are on the path to becoming a master of your craft—embodying the spirit of the Zen archer with each keystroke. Embrace this journey, and let your mastery shine brightly in the coding world.

10. The Philosophical Core: Zen and Mastery

10.1. The Role of Zen in Mastery

The integration of Zen principles into the mastery of coding reflects a profound journey toward achieving both technical excellence and personal growth. Zen is not merely an abstract philosophy; it manifests in very tangible practices that enhance focus, clarity, and intentionality in coding. As we explore the intricate relationship between Zen and mastery in coding, we uncover the layered facets of learning, development, and the continuous evolution of skills.

To start, the essence of mastery in any discipline, including coding, parallels the Zen practice of mindfulness and presence. The journey toward becoming a "master" coder is not marked solely by the number of languages learned or frameworks mastered, but by the dedication to continuous improvement and self-awareness. Code mastery involves a constant cycle of learning, application, reflection, and refocusing—an iterative process that encourages coders to embrace challenges as opportunities for growth. Much like a Zen practitioner who dedicates time to refining their techniques, coders must invest in the art of programming, consciously seeking to deepen their understanding and enhance their skillset.

Central to this journey is the realization that coding is an art form as much as it is a technical skill. Each line of code represents not only a command to the computer but also a reflection of a coder's thoughts, creativity, and problem-solving abilities. When applying Zen principles, coders can learn to approach their work with a sense of purpose and creativity, leading to innovative solutions that embody both functionality and elegance. This combination of artistry and technology allows coders to strike a harmonious balance between these seemingly disparate realms.

Another core aspect of the connection between Zen and coding mastery is the importance of purpose. Identifying the "why" behind your coding efforts cultivates an intrinsic sense of motivation. Understanding how your coding impacts users, projects, or the broader community fosters a deeper emotional connection to your work, driving you to pursue excellence. When coders see their work as contributing to the greater good, the act of programming transforms from a rote task to a meaningful endeavor. This aligns with Zen's emphasis on understanding one's place in the world and acting with intention toward achieving harmony.

In the context of community, Zen principles underscore the importance of connection, collaboration, and shared learning. The tech community thrives on mutual support, knowledge exchange, and collaboration, creating an environment in which both experienced and novice coders can flourish. By participating in discussions, forums, and collaborative coding sessions, coders can embrace the Zen teaching of interconnectedness. Communities built on empathy, understanding, and encouragement empower individuals to pursue mastery, share insights, and collectively elevate the coding landscape.

Reflect on the methodologies that foster mastery in coding. Incorporating regular practices of reflection, such as journaling experiences, analyzing successes and failures, and documenting learning journeys, leads to a clearer understanding of both strengths and areas for growth. In a similar vein, demonstration of mastery is often revealed through how challenges are approached and resolved. Coders who embody perseverance, patience, and adaptability mirror the values inherent in Zen philosophy and position themselves to evolve continuously while striving towards excellence.

Ultimately, the pursuit of mastery within coding is a dynamic, ongoing endeavor—an invitation to embrace both the technical and philosophical elements of the craft. By intertwining Zen principles into everyday coding practices, coders are invited to engage deeply with their work, cultivate resilience, foster collaboration, and remain open to growth. This journey, enriched by self-awareness and mindful practices, enables mastery to flourish, transforming coders into adept practitioners who not only hit the targets of technical excellence but do so with grace and intention.

In closing, the synthesis of Zen philosophy with coding practice offers a path toward holistic mastery—one that transcends technology to embrace the values of clarity, simplicity, and compassion. As you advance in your coding journey, let these principles guide your actions and decisions, allowing for a meaningful experience that celebrates the art of coding as both an individual pursuit and a collective mission. Embrace the way of the Zen archer, and strive continually towards your coding goals with mindful precision and purpose.

10.2. Mastery as a Lifelong Journey

Mastery is often perceived as a destination—a pinnacle achieved through experience, skill development, and proficiency. However, true mastery, especially in the realm of coding with Emacs, should be recognized as a lifelong journey. This journey is not linear; it is filled with twists, turns, setbacks, and breakthroughs. It mirrors the commitment of a Zen practitioner who commits to daily practice and reflects upon each moment with presence and intention.

At the core of this journey lies the understanding that mastery is not merely about acquiring knowledge; it is about cultivating wisdom through experience. Each project you undertake, each bug you fix, and each line of code you write contributes to a larger tapestry of growth. By immersing yourself in the Zen principles of mindfulness, patience, and presence, you embark on an unpredictable yet transformative path where every encounter is an opportunity for learning and reflection.

In the context of coding, this journey begins with the realization that perfection is not the goal—progress is. Embrace the notion that each iteration of your code is an evolving thought, a moment in your development as a coder. Just as a Zen archer practices repeatedly to hone their skills without the expectation of perfection, you too must cultivate a spirit of compassion for yourself. Allow for mistakes and setbacks to be integral parts of the journey. Reflect on them, understand the lessons embedded in each, and continue to move forward with grace.

As you navigate your coding journey, take the time to focus on the process rather than solely on the end result. Devote yourself to the act of coding with intentionality, embracing each keystroke. Immerse yourself in the rhythm of writing code as you would in a meditation. Maintain engagement with the present moment, recognizing the beauty of creation in each function and the elegance of solution-building. This mindful approach fosters creativity and sparks inspiration that goes beyond coding itself.

The landscape of technology is ever-evolving; new languages, frameworks, and methodologies emerge regularly. To maintain relevance and growth, a commitment to continuous learning is essential. Approach your coding journey with an insatiable curiosity, exploring new paradigms and methodologies that stretch your capabilities. Engage in coding communities where knowledge is shared freely, enriching your journey with insights from peers. Participate in webinars, workshops, and conferences to expand not only your technical skills but also your understanding of the cultural and ethical implications of coding.

Empowerment also comes through reflection. Set aside time to evaluate what you've learned after completing projects or reaching milestones. Ask yourself critical questions: What worked well? What would I change if I could do it again? How did I grow as a coder through this experience? By actively engaging in reflective practices, you deepen your understanding of your craft, allowing for continued evolution that aligns with your personal and professional goals.

Furthermore, cultivate a sense of community within your coding practice. Engage with fellow coders not just for knowledge exchange but also for support and encouragement on this journey. Surrounding yourself with like-minded individuals amplifies your enthusiasm, fosters accountability, and creates a collaborative atmosphere where mastery can flourish.

As you develop your skills, remain aware of the balance between technical proficiency and the soft skills that enhance your professional presence. Adaptability, effective communication, and empathy toward users and teammates are essential components that lead to successful collaboration and contribute to a holistic understanding of mastery in coding.

In conclusion, mastering coding with Emacs—and indeed any skill—requires the commitment to view it as a lifelong journey. Embrace the principles of mindfulness, reflection, and continuous learning while recognizing the value inherent in each experience. Approach your coding endeavors as a Zen practitioner would, allowing each obstacle to contribute to your growth and each success to deepen your understanding of your craft. Celebrate your progress with gratitude, and remember that the true essence of mastery lies in the journey itself, continually evolving in the pursuit of knowledge, skill, and understanding. Let this path guide you as you navigate the world of coding, empowering yourself to express creativity and innovation through the elegant dance of your code.

10.3. The Intersection of Art and Technology

In a rapidly evolving digital landscape, the intersection of art and technology offers a fertile ground for innovative expression and creative problem-solving. This section invites you to explore how these seemingly disparate realms come together in the realm of coding, specifically through the lens of Emacs, a tool that epitomizes the fusion of artistry and engineering.

Consider coding as an art form where each line written is not merely functional but also an expression of creativity, intention, and design. Just as a painter applies strokes to canvas with careful consideration of color, form, and composition, programmers write code with an understanding of structure, logic, and purpose. Successful coding transcends assembling functional requirements; it demands an aesthetic quality where the elegance of the solution and the clarity of the implementation coexist harmoniously.

For many developers, coding challenges can evoke frustrations and blockages that inhibit creativity. It is in these moments that the philosophical underpinning of art—inspiration—becomes crucial. The ability to step back, breathe, and approach problems from new angles allows for clarity and creativity to flourish. Engage in practices from the Zen tradition, such as mindfulness and meditation, to facilitate this shift in perspective. By cultivating mindfulness, coders can better navigate stress, enhance focus, and spark innovative thinking when faced with difficulties.

When we consider the tools we employ, Emacs stands out as an edit-energy powerhouse that emphasizes artistry in coding. Its extensibility and customization capabilities empower developers to tailor their environments to reflect individual preferences and workflows. The very act of configuring Emacs—from selecting themes to installing plugins—is akin to an artist arranging their palette, selecting the right brushes, and preparing the canvas. This personalized interaction fortifies the connection between coder and tool, allowing creative expressions to emerge through thoughtful configurations.

Furthermore, engaging with the community around Emacs enhances the artistic aspect of coding. Much like artists sharing techniques and critiques, coders can engage in knowledge exchange, discussing plugins or workflows that foster collective growth. This collaborative spirit leads to the evolution of new ideas, novel plugins, and innovative applications, all of which contribute to the shared tapestry of the coding universe.

As we delve deeper into the realm of artistic expression, it is essential to embrace playfulness and experimentation. Just as artists take creative liberties and diverge from conventional forms, coders can benefit from adopting an experimental mindset. Embrace side projects, hackathons, or creative coding challenges where the primary aim is not the end product but the journey itself. Such explorations push boundaries, inspire growth, and ignite the creative spark that often leads to breakthroughs in more structured coding environments.

It's essential to acknowledge that the art of coding is not limited to written code alone. Documentation, code organization, and collaborative practices are also facets of this artistry. Well-documented code transcends mere functionality, imparting narrative and context that elevate understanding for both the author and those collaborating on the project. Much like an artist sharing insights into their creative process through captions or artist statements, detailed comments and documentation breathe life into the code, allowing others to appreciate not just the "what," but the "why" behind each decision.

Lastly, the cultivated relationship between art and technology urges coders to close the loop of creativity by reflecting on their work. After completing a project, take the time to assess the decisions made throughout the process. What creative avenues did you explore? Did the implementation reflect a balance between form and function? This reflective practice fosters growth, allowing you to draw connections between technical execution and artistic expression, shaping your ongoing journey toward mastery.

In summary, the intersection of art and technology within the coding world inspires a creative approach to problem-solving, engagement, and expression. By embracing the principles of artistic thought, building personalized Emacs environments, engaging with the community, experimenting boldly, and prioritizing reflection, coders can cultivate a rich and fulfilling relationship with their craft. Let this exploration of artistry within the technical realm guide you as you dive deeper into the world of coding, enabling you to hit the targets of creativity and innovation with each keystroke.

10.4. Finding Purpose in Coding

Finding purpose in coding is a profound exploration that intertwines technical proficiency with intrinsic motivation, resulting in a meaningful and impactful coding journey. In our fast-paced, technology-driven world, it's not uncommon for coders to lose sight of why they started programming in the first place. This subchapter invites you to reexamine the motivations behind your coding efforts and discover how you can align your technical skills with a greater purpose that resonates deeply within you.

At the outset of this journey, take a moment to reflect on what coding means to you. Is it merely a means to an end—a job that pays the bills —or does it serve a deeper significance in your life? This reflection provides a powerful springboard for uncovering your unique motivations. Perhaps coding grants you the opportunity to create, innovate, or solve problems that matter to you, or it may be a vehicle for empowering others through your work. Understanding your personal relationship with coding is a crucial step in harnessing your passion and ultimately shaping your purpose.

As you contemplate your purpose in coding, consider the broader impact that technology has on society. Throughout history, advancements in technology have transformed lives, bridged gaps, and increased efficiency across countless sectors. Reflect on how your coding contributions can serve not only individual users but also communities, organizations, and society at large. When you recognize that your work can drive positive change, the act of coding acquires significance beyond the screen, becoming a form of artistic expression that resonates deeply with your values.

Next, actively engage with projects that align with your passions and ideals. Seek opportunities to work on open-source projects that resonate with your interests or develop prototypes for products that fulfill a need you deeply believe in. Contributing to technology that enhances education, improves accessibility, or addresses environmental issues can be immensely fulfilling. Channeling your coding efforts toward initiatives that align with your values provides a profound sense of purpose, fueling your commitment and effort to cultivate excellence in your craft.

In addition to personal projects, collaborating with others can refine your sense of purpose in coding. Engage in communities where sharing ideas and experiences fosters collective growth and motivation. When you work alongside like-minded individuals who share your passion for coding and the potential of technology, you tap into a wellspring of inspiration and accountability. Seek mentorship opportunities, join coding patagonia meetups, or participate in hackathons.

This interconnectedness elevates your coding journey beyond individual pursuits and reinforces the notion that your work contributes to a larger narrative of progress and innovation.

Moreover, remember that your purpose in coding can evolve over time. As you gain experience, explore new technologies, and take on diverse coding challenges, your motivations may shift. Embrace this fluidity; allow yourself the grace to recalibrate your goals as you grow. Reflect on your coding journey regularly to ensure that your efforts continue to align with your evolving vision. This adaptability reflects a mindful approach coherent with the Zen practice of being present in the moment and acknowledging the transformative nature of the path ahead.

Finding purpose in your coding journey also beckons an element of compassion. Practice empathy in your coding efforts, especially when developing solutions for users. Approach your code with an intention to serve, ensuring that it resonates with users' needs and aspirations. Understanding the human element behind your coding work enriches your creations, reminding you that technology exists not solely for technical perfection but for enhancing the human experience.

In conclusion, finding purpose in coding is a multifaceted journey that encourages deep introspection, engagement with community, and adaptability. Recognize the impact that your coding efforts can have on society, seek projects that resonate with your values, and embrace collaboration with like-minded individuals. This pursuit of purpose transforms the act of coding into a meaningful endeavor that nurtures not only your technical skills but also your personal and professional fulfillment. Allow this journey toward purpose to guide your coding practice and propel you toward continued excellence in your craft. As you navigate this path, remember that every keystroke is a step toward enriching the world with your unique contributions.

10.5. Connecting with Community

In a rapidly evolving digital landscape, the act of coding transcends mere technical proficiency to become a holistic practice deeply embedded in community and collaboration. This subchapter explores the essence of "Connecting with Community" in the context of Emacs coding, emphasizing the vital role that engagement with like-minded individuals plays in one's professional and personal growth. Just as a Zen archer finds support and inspiration in their fellow archers, coders can cultivate an enriching environment through mutual connection, leading to shared knowledge and collaborative creativity.

Community engagement begins with the recognition that coding is inherently a collaborative process. The complexity and demands of contemporary software development often require diverse perspectives and skills. In this light, being part of a coding community not only broadens your knowledge base but also facilitates connection with others who are similarly passionate about technology. Such engagement fosters an atmosphere rich in creativity, learning, and exploration, encouraging individuals to share challenges, insights, and innovations.

Online platforms and forums dedicated to Emacs can facilitate this connection. Engage actively in communities such as Reddit's r/emacs or Emacs Stack Exchange, where knowledge is freely exchanged, and questions are welcomed. By participating in discussions surrounding code principles, configurations, and troubleshooting, you not only deepen your own learning but also contribute to a culture of shared understanding. Empathy and kindness within these interactions resonate with the essence of Zen practice, enriching the community and creating a supportive network of coders.

Moreover, attending local or virtual meetups and conferences can serve as powerful means to connect with fellow Emacs users and coders alike. Events focused on specific technologies allow for direct engagement with peers, sparking conversations that can lead to partnerships, knowledge sharing, and inspiration. These gatherings not only foster a sense of belonging but can also serve as platforms to showcase your work—a practice that strengthens collaboration as community members learn from each other's experiences.

When engaging with the coding community, consider collaborating on open-source projects or contributing to existing ones. Open-source initiatives offer ample opportunities to learn from seasoned developers while positively impacting the broader community. As you contribute to projects, you'll gain insight into various coding styles, practices, and challenges faced by other developers. This experience is invaluable; similar to an archer learning through practice within their community, your skills will naturally evolve through shared coding experiences.

In addition to formal coding communities, fostering relationships with colleagues can enhance personal growth and codifying Zen practices within your work culture. Encourage open communication within your team, creating a culture that values inclusivity and vulnerability. Team members should feel comfortable reaching out for help, sharing their experiences, and seeking feedback, thereby building a strong support network. A collective approach to coding enhances problem-solving, celebrates successes, and motivates individuals to keep pushing their boundaries.

Incorporating mentorship into this framework can further bolster community connections. Seek out senior developers or seasoned Emacs users who are willing to guide and support you on your coding journey. Alternatively, as you gain proficiency, consider mentoring newcomers yourself. This reciprocal relationship nurtures a culture of empathy and learning, reinforcing the Zen principle of collective growth. It fosters connections that extend beyond hierarchies, creating an interconnected community where everyone plays a vital role.

Lastly, remember that community contribution extends beyond coding. Getting involved in discussions on best practices, ethical coding, or activism in the tech space can deepen your engagement and provide a sense of purpose that transcends individual practice. Embracing the idea of responsibility toward the community allows for a more holistic approach to coding that embodies the teachings of Zen —recognizing how individual actions contribute to the collective.

In conclusion, connecting with community is a fundamental aspect of the coding journey that can provide profound benefits for personal and professional development. Engaging with fellow coders, participating in open-source projects, nurturing relationships with colleagues, embracing mentorship, and contributing to broader discussions all create a rich tapestry of shared knowledge and support. By drawing upon the principles of Zen in fostering connection, you embody the spirit of the Zen archer—relying on the strength of the community to enhance your practice and navigate the intricate world of coding with clarity and purpose. Embrace the journey of connectivity, and let the collaborative spirit enrich your coding experience.

11. Maintaining a Zen Edge in a Fast-Paced World

11.1. Staying Grounded Amidst Distractions

Staying grounded amidst distractions is essential for maintaining focus and achieving productivity in the often chaotic world of coding. In a digital landscape filled with notifications, constant interruptions, and the pressure of deadlines, mastering the art of concentration becomes vital. This subchapter offers practical strategies rooted in mindfulness to help you maintain clarity and purpose, ensuring that your coding sessions are focused and fulfilling.

To begin with, it is crucial to create an environment that minimizes distractions. Just as an archer chooses a quiet and serene setting to perfect their aim, your workspace should reflect a similarly focused atmosphere. This begins with your physical surroundings—eliminate clutter and unnecessary items that could draw your attention away from your code. Ensure that your desk is organized, with tools and resources easily accessible. Pay attention to lighting; a well-lit space, free from glare, enhances focus and reduces eye strain.

Additionally, consider your digital environment. Close any non-essential applications and browser tabs during coding sessions. Use tools that can block distracting websites or notifications that pull you away from your work. Embrace tools such as 'Do Not Disturb' settings on your devices to minimize interruptions, creating a barrier that guards your focus. Setting boundaries around your work hours also communicates to others that you are in a dedicated coding space, much like an archer instructing their peers to remain quiet during practice.

Establishing a focused coding routine plays a vital role in maintaining concentration. Embody a predictable structure for your work sessions that includes set intervals for coding and brief periods for breaks. Techniques like the Pomodoro Technique, which advocates for working in focused bursts followed by short breaks, encourage sustained attention. During these focus intervals, commit to immersing yourself fully in the task at hand, resisting the urge to check emails or social media. This defined routine cultivates a sense of purpose, allowing you to progress steadily through your work.

Mindfulness practices can further enhance your ability to stay grounded during coding. Take the time at the beginning of each session to engage in a brief mindfulness exercise—this could be guided breathing, meditation, or even a few moments of visualization. Visualize yourself in a state of calm, focused concentration as you embark on your coding journey. This exercise primes your mind to remain present and attentive, helping you to direct your energy toward the task before you, just as the Zen archer visualizes their shot before releasing the arrow.

When distractions inevitably arise, it is essential to have strategies in place that allow you to regain focus quickly. Rather than letting interruptions fester in your mind, practice acknowledging them without judgment. If a distracting thought surfaces—be it a pending task or personal concern—take a moment to recognize it and gently redirect your attention back to your coding. A useful technique is to keep a notepad nearby, allowing you to jot down distracting thoughts quickly while assuring your mind that they will be addressed later. This approach gives you permission to set aside those thoughts while remaining immersed in your coding session.

Cultivating self-compassion is another core principle that should guide you in staying grounded. Understand that distractions are a normal part of the human experience. Practice kindness towards yourself, recognizing that it is okay to falter occasionally. Maintaining a non-critical perspective allows you to focus on what you can control —your reactions and choices—and promotes resilience in your coding practice.

Establishing clear goals and intentions for each coding session can also help maintain focus. Before diving into your work, clarify what you hope to accomplish, whether it's completing a specific feature, debugging code, or conducting research on a new technology. This clarity acts as a guiding light throughout your coding session, reminding you of your objective and reducing the likelihood of being drawn into distractions that may arise.

Finally, encourage a culture of respect within your coding community and work environment. When working in teams or collaborative settings, establish norms that promote mindfulness and minimize disturbances. Encourage peers to communicate efficiently and respect boundaries when it comes to focus time. Just as an archer relies on the support and understanding of fellow team members, creating a collaborative environment that values collective focus can reduce distractions and enhance overall productivity.

In conclusion, maintaining focus amidst distractions is a skill that can be developed through mindfulness, intentionality, and supportive practices. By creating a conducive physical and digital workspace, establishing a structured routine, engaging in mindfulness exercises, fostering self-compassion, setting clear goals, and encouraging respect within teams, you can navigate the challenges of coding with clarity and purpose. Embrace these strategies to stay grounded, enabling you to immerse yourself in your coding endeavors fully and hit your targets with precision and confidence, much like a Zen archer poised to release their arrow.

11.2. The Art of Slow Coding

The art of slow coding is a practice steeped in mindfulness, reflection, and intentionality, which resonates deeply with the principles of Zen. In a world where speed often seems to dictate success, the concept of slow coding encourages developers to step back, assess their approach, and immerse themselves fully in the craft of coding. This method not only fosters greater insight into one's work but leads to the production of cleaner, more maintainable code — a vital outcome for any coding endeavor.

At the heart of slow coding lies the recognition that true mastery of any craft, including programming, cannot be rushed. Just as a Zen archer patiently practices their aim, anticipating and embracing each moment, so too should coders adopt a measured pace when tackling coding tasks. The journey to mastery is not instantaneous; it demands time, focus, and, above all, an appreciation for the artistic nature of the work being done.

Setting clear intentions at the outset of each coding session is paramount. Before diving into a task, take time to contemplate the goals for that session. What problems are you trying to solve? What features are you implementing? By establishing awareness and clarity of purpose, you can center yourself and create a nurturing environment for focused coding. This deliberate approach fosters a sense of calm, enabling you to engage deeply with your work without the incessant pressure to hurry.

One effective technique in slow coding is to break tasks into smaller, more manageable segments. Instead of attempting to tackle a large project in one go, set incremental goals that allow you to focus on specific components at a time. This method mirrors the practice of an archer taking careful aim before releasing their shot—by concentrating on the individual elements, you can cultivate quality and precision in your code. Celebrate these small successes along the way; acknowledging progress fosters motivation and reinforces the value of slow, deliberate work.

In addition to breaking tasks down, adopt practices of reflection throughout the coding process. After writing a section of code, take a pause to review and assess your work. What decisions did you make, and why? Are there opportunities for improvement? This introspective moment allows you to learn from each piece of code, reinforcing the notion that coding is an evolving art form requiring continuous refinement.

Integrate periods of rest into your coding rhythm as well. Similar to the way an archer might need to step back after several rounds to reassess their practice, taking breaks allows your mind to recharge and your focus to restore. These moments away from the screen can inspire new ideas and perspectives upon returning to your work.

Consider incorporating techniques like the Pomodoro Technique as part of your slow coding practice—short, focused bursts of work followed by intentional pauses can enhance overall productivity while maintaining a priority on mental well-being.

Moreover, be mindful of the code you write, crafting it with the same care an artist would employ when creating a piece of art. Embrace readability, simplicity, and elegance—strive to write code that is not only functional but also clear and maintainable. This principle emphasizes the distinction between writing code and creating software that provides a positive experience for those who will read or interact with it in the future.

Collaboration can also thrive within the slow coding framework. By taking your time and allowing space for discussion or peer review, you create a culture that values thoughtful contributions over hastily produced code. Emphasizing slow coding principles within a collaborative environment fosters a spirit of respect and support, allowing team members to engage each other's thoughts and insights consciously.

Lastly, embrace a mindset that revels in the journey of coding rather than solely focusing on the end result. It is the discipline of practice, the exploration of ideas, and the process of creating that reveal growth and mastery over time. By cultivating this perspective, you'll find that slow coding becomes not just a strategy but a deeply enriching experience—a journey through which you come to appreciate both the craft of coding and the learning that arises from each moment spent engaged in it.

In summary, the art of slow coding embodies the Zen principles of mindfulness, intentionality, and reflection. By adopting a measured approach to coding—establishing clarity of purpose, breaking tasks into manageable segments, integrating reflection, prioritizing mental well-being, crafting readable code, embracing collaboration, and celebrating the journey—you can transform your coding practice into a rewarding and fulfilling endeavor. With each line of code written in this manner, you channel the essence of a Zen archer, drawing upon patience, clarity, and purpose to hit the coding bullseye with precision.

11.3. Preventing Burnout

Preventing burnout is essential in maintaining the balance between a fulfilling coding practice and personal well-being. In the fast-paced world of technology, where the expectations are high and deadlines loom large, the risk of burnout is ever-present. However, by incorporating Zen principles into your coding routine and overall approach to work, you can create a sustainable practice that promotes resilience, clarity, and joy in your craft.

To begin, it is crucial to recognize the early signs of burnout. Symptoms may include chronic fatigue, decreased motivation, irritability, or a growing sense of disconnection from your work. Often, these feelings stem from the relentless pace and pressure that accompany coding projects. By cultivating self-awareness and tuning into your mental and physical states, you can better identify when these signs begin to surface. This practice embodies the Zen principle of mindfulness, where being present and attuned to your internal landscape allows you to respond proactively to emerging stress rather than reactively succumbing to overwhelm.

Once you become aware of the signs, it is vital to implement strategies that promote balance and well-being. Establishing clear boundaries between work and personal life is fundamental to preventing burnout. Set defined working hours, ensuring that coding doesn't spill over into personal time. Respecting these boundaries allows you to recharge and cultivate hobbies and interests outside of coding, much like an archer who takes time away from practice to maintain a well-rounded lifestyle. This balance fosters resilience, enabling you to return to your coding projects refreshed and engaged.

Another effective strategy is to integrate regular breaks into your coding sessions. Embrace practices such as the Pomodoro Technique, which suggests working in focused intervals followed by short

132

breaks. Stepping away from your screen for brief restorative periods allows your mind to recuperate and enhances focus when you return to coding. During these breaks, engage in activities that bring you joy and relaxation—be it a walk outside, a few moments of deep breathing, or simply stretching your body. By giving your mind and body the care they need, you foster a healthier relationship with coding that diminishes stress.

Fostering a supportive work environment plays a crucial role in preventing burnout. Engage openly with colleagues about workloads, project expectations, and any struggles you may encounter. Establishing a culture of empathy and understanding nurtures vulnerability, allowing team members to express concerns and seek assistance without fear of judgment. Much like archers who support one another during practice, fostering a collaborative atmosphere can lessen the pressure felt individually, creating a community that thrives on mutual encouragement.

Incorporating mindfulness practices can also serve as a potent countermeasure to burnout. Dedicate time to engage in mindfulness techniques such as meditation, deep breathing exercises, or even mindful coding, where you approach your programming tasks with intention and awareness. By immersing yourself fully in your work while remaining attuned to your thoughts and emotions, you can transform the coding experience into one of focus and presence, minimizing stress and enhancing outcomes.

Regularly reviewing your workload and responsibilities can also fortify your defenses against burnout. Periodically assess the projects and tasks on your plate to ensure that they align with your values, capacities, and long-term goals. If you find yourself overwhelmed by commitments, don't hesitate to delegate tasks or communicate with your team about redistributing workloads. Just as an archer would adjust their focus on the range depending on external factors, adapting your workload is a vital part of maintaining harmony.

Taking time for self-care is crucial, especially when burnout looms. Engage in activities that rejuvenate you outside of coding—be it exercise, creative pursuits, or community involvement. Nurturing your overall well-being ensures you remain emotionally and physically fit to tackle coding challenges with renewed vigor. Remember, fostering this balance enriches your coding practice and reinforces your connection to your work.

Finally, embrace the journey of coding as a continuous learning experience. Shift your mindset from viewing setbacks or challenges as sources of frustration to recognizing them as opportunities for growth. Adopting a growth mentality positions you to flourish amidst pressures while reinforcing the notion of coding as both an art and a discipline.

In conclusion, preventing burnout through a Zen approach requires self-awareness, clear boundaries, mindfulness practices, supportive culture, and a commitment to self-care. By implementing these strategies, you can cultivate a coding practice that marries productivity with well-being, enabling you to approach each coding endeavor with clarity, focus, and joy. Embrace this holistic approach and watch how your coding journey flourishes, allowing you to hit the bullseye in your craft with resilience and purpose.

11.4. Balancing Professional and Personal Life

In today's fast-paced technological landscape, the challenge of balancing professional obligations with personal life has become increasingly salient for coders and programmers. Just as the Zen archer must maintain focus and clarity while navigating the complexities of a shooting range, coders must also seek equilibrium amidst the myriad demands of their careers and personal aspirations. This balance is not just desirable but crucial for enhancing productivity, creativity, and overall well-being.

To forge this harmony, it's essential to first acknowledge the distinct realms of professional and personal responsibilities. Your professional life encompasses work obligations, projects, deadlines, and the dynamics of team collaboration. Conversely, personal life encompasses family, friends, hobbies, self-care, and downtime. The interplay between these spheres can create tension; when work demands encroach on personal time, stress and burnout may follow. Conversely, when personal concerns disrupt work focus, productivity can suffer.

Establishing boundaries serves as the foundation for achieving balance. Define clear work hours and personal time, ensuring that once you leave your workspace or shut down your computer, you transition into a space dedicated to relaxation and rejuvenation. Communicate these boundaries to colleagues and family members, fostering an environment of respect around your time. By setting these boundaries, you create a psychological buffer that allows you to immerse yourself fully in either professional or personal settings, mirroring the focus a Zen archer maintains on the target.

Time management plays a pivotal role in achieving this balance. Utilize techniques such as the Pomodoro Technique, where you work in focused intervals followed by short breaks. This structure not only enhances productivity but allows you to allocate blocks of time for personal activities, ensuring you prioritize both your professional responsibilities and personal fulfillment. When you view coding sessions as opportunities for concentrated work, and personal time as essential for recuperation, you cultivate a rhythm that mitigates the risk of burnout while maximizing focus.

Mindfulness practices can substantially enhance your ability to balance these aspects of life. Engaging with mindfulness—such as meditation, deep-breathing exercises, or mindful coding—can help anchor your attention and promote a state of presence, allowing you to be more attuned to your thoughts and feelings. When distractions arise—be it a frustrating bug or personal stress—mindfulness can guide you to respond with clarity rather than react impulsively. This practice fosters emotional resilience, enabling you to address challenges in both your professional and personal spheres proactively.

In the spirit of Zen, prioritize self-care and personal pursuits. Investing in activities and hobbies that bring joy and relaxation can reinvigorate your sense of self outside of work. Whether it's engaging in physical exercise, pursuing an artistic endeavor, or simply enjoying time with loved ones, nurturing these elements of your personal life reinforces your overall well-being. Just as an archer must care for their body and mind to perform effectively, coders must prioritize self-care to maintain their best performance.

Furthermore, embrace flexibility within your balance. As projects fluctuate, unexpected demands may arise that disrupt your carefully crafted equilibrium. Acknowledge that achieving perfect balance at all times may be unrealistic; instead, cultivate a responsive mindset that allows you to adapt and adjust your priorities as needed. When work demands peak, be prepared to lean into professional commitments, but also ensure that you carve out small moments for self-care and relaxation wherever possible.

Lastly, cultivate a supportive network. Foster relationships within your professional environment that encourage open dialogue regarding workload, personal well-being, and boundaries. Collaboration and community among your peers can create a culture of understanding, empathy, and support—ensuring that everyone's individual needs are recognized and respected. Much like an archer seeking guidance from fellow practitioners, your network can offer valuable support and insight that enhances the balance between professional and personal life.

In conclusion, balancing professional and personal life within the coding landscape requires intentionality, mindfulness, and flexibility. By establishing boundaries, managing time effectively, embracing mindfulness practices, prioritizing self-care, and nurturing supportive relationships, you can foster harmony between these two vital aspects of your life. Embrace the journey of seeking balance with compassion and acceptance, and allow it to enhance your experience as both a coder and an individual. Ultimately, by hitting the target of equilibrium, you can thrive in both realms, achieving not only professional success but also personal fulfillment—a true testament to the art of the Zen archer.

11.5. Embracing Change with Grace

Embracing change with grace is an essential practice in the journey of coding, particularly within the flexible and dynamic environment of Emacs. As coders, we frequently encounter shifts in technology, updates to tools, changes in team structures, and evolving project requirements. Just like a Zen archer adapts their aim to account for variable conditions—such as wind, distance, and the ever-changing nature of the target—coders must cultivate a mindset that allows them to navigate change seamlessly and with intent.

To begin with, embracing change with grace requires a mental framework that recognizes change as an opportunity for growth rather than a hindrance. Adopting a growth mindset is crucial. This mindset enables you to view challenges as learning experiences that contribute to personal and professional development. Each change, whether it's adopting a new programming language, implementing a new tool, or adjusting to new team dynamics, can be seen as a stepping stone on your path to mastery. Much like an archer who studies each shot they take—regardless of whether it hits the target—coders can track the lessons learned from every adaptation and adjustment, improving their skills and resilience through reflection and analysis.

Preparation is also key to managing change effectively. When you know a significant change is forthcoming—whether it's a shift in project direction or the introduction of a new language—take proactive steps to familiarize yourself with the new landscape. Engage in research, attend workshops, explore relevant documentation, and practice using new tools or languages in small projects. This proactive stance empowers you to mitigate feelings of uncertainty and overwhelm, allowing you to approach changes with confidence rather than apprehension. Like an archer tuning their equipment before a competition, adequately preparing for the upcoming adaptations equips you with the tools necessary for success.

Additionally, maintaining flexibility during transitions is paramount. Change often requires unexpected adjustments, and the ability to pivot when necessary allows coders to manage new information or challenges without losing sight of their goals. Create a culture of adaptability within your coding practice—embrace the idea that it's not just about rigidly following a predetermined path but about being open to exploring diverse avenues and solutions. This adaptability is a healthy tactic for dealing with both minor and major shifts, enabling you to move forward without resistance.

In cultivating this flexible mindset, it's also important to institute regular reflection and feedback loops. After experiencing a change—whether personal or technical—set aside time to evaluate how it was navigated. What went well during the process? What challenges arose and how were they addressed? Reflecting on these experiences cultivates a deeper awareness of your strengths and areas for improvement, reinforcing your ability to embrace future changes gracefully. Think of it similarly to recording shots taken during archery practice; noting where adjustments were successful can inform future attempts in much the same way.

Embracing a community context can also help facilitate smoother transitions. Other coders may face similar shifts, and discussing challenges with peers fosters a sense of solidarity and shared experiences. Leaning on your community not only offers individual support but allows you to pool resources and knowledge, reinforcing the notion that no coder is isolated in their journey.

Moreover, approaching changes with a sense of curiosity can transform the experience entirely. Instead of focusing solely on the end result or worrying about performance, approach changes as invitations to explore, understand, and innovate. This creativity-like mindset is often where some of the most unexpected and brilliant solutions emerge.

Lastly, maintaining a sense of compassion for yourself is crucial when navigating changes. Understand that adaptation is a process that may involve missteps along the way. Much like the Zen archer who may miss the target on occasion, remember that these moments are not failures but learning opportunities that contribute to a richer understanding of your craft.

In conclusion, embracing change with grace in coding is an art that requires mindfulness, adaptability, and a willingness to grow. By adopting a growth mindset, preparing adequately for impending changes, remaining flexible in your approach, engaging in regular reflection, fostering community support, embracing curiosity, and practicing self-compassion, you can navigate the often tumultuous waters of coding with poise and clarity. By embodying these principles, you can emerge stronger, more innovative, and ever more proficient, positioning yourself to achieve your coding goals—just as the Zen archer continually seeks the perfect shot, grounded in practice and awareness.

12. Exploring Advanced Emacs Techniques

12.1. Harnessing Advanced Commands

Harnessing advanced commands within Emacs is akin to unearthing the depths of a hidden wellspring of knowledge and power—drawing from an expansive array of functionalities designed to enhance productivity and workflow efficiency. Just as a Zen archer hones their techniques to navigate complex shooting conditions and improve accuracy, mastering Emacs commands allows you to streamline your coding practices and navigate the intricacies of your projects with grace and precision.

To begin your journey into advanced commands, it's essential to familiarize yourself with the command execution framework in Emacs. The primary method for invoking commands is through the M-x prompt. This powerful tool allows you to tap into Emacs's extensive library of functions and commands. Whenever you find yourself in need of a specific functionality or command, simply invoke M-x followed by the command name. For instance, entering M-x describe-function provides valuable documentation about any predefined command or function, ensuring that you remain informed about the capabilities of Emacs.

One of the core advanced commands to integrate into your workflow is M-!, which allows you to execute shell commands directly within Emacs. This command opens a terminal within your editing environment, enabling you to run system commands or scripts without the need to switch contexts. For example, you might use M-! git status to quickly check the status of your Git repository while coding. The ability to interact seamlessly with your operating system through Emacs removes friction from your workflow, allowing for fluid transitions between coding and command execution.

Incorporating keyboard shortcuts is critical for harnessing the full potential of advanced commands. Customizing keybindings to fit your workflow not only reduces the time spent navigating your environment but also empowers you to execute commands with precision and speed. Use the following command to bind a specific function to a key combination:

```
(global-set-key (kbd "C-c g") 'magit-status)
```

This line binds the `magit-status` command to `C-c g`, allowing you to access Git status effortlessly with a single keystroke. This practice reflects how Zen archers perfect synchronization between their movements, emphasizing the precision of their draws and releases.

To further enhance your skills, engage in the use of registers—a powerful feature in Emacs that allows you to store and retrieve text snippets, positions, or rectangles with ease. By employing registers, you can save the current cursor position using `C-x r SPC` (register name), then return to that position later by invoking `C-x r j` (register name). This enables you to navigate large codebases efficiently, enhancing your productivity and focus while coding.

Another advanced command that deserves exploration is `C-u`. This universal argument command modifies how the next command behaves based on the value passed to it. For example, if you call `C-u 3 C-n`, you will navigate three lines down instead of just one. Embracing the flexibility of the universal argument empowers you to customize your interactions with Emacs, allowing for rapid movements through your code and enhancing your workflow in a manner akin to an archer adjusting their stance based on conditions.

Additionally, mastering multiple cursors is a game-changing advancement in productivity for Emacs users. With the `multiple-cursors` package, you can simultaneously edit multiple lines of code or create selections across various instances of a word or phrase. By utilizing commands such as `C-S-c C-S-c`, you can activate multiple cursors, giving you the capability to edit efficiently and effectively —this mirrors the way an archer may embrace varying techniques based on their target.

As your exploration continues, consider the use of `Isearch`, an incremental search functionality that enriches your text navigation experience. By invoking `C-s`, you can search text within your files as you type—making it easy to find specific functions, comments, or variables without disrupting your flow. Coupled with the ability to use C-r for reverse search, Isearch enhances your ability to explore your codebase with great precision.

Define custom commands or functions to automate repetitive tasks, allowing you to relinquish mundane actions that detract from your creative engagement. Emacs Lisp offers a powerful framework for creating reusable functions according to your needs. With each custom command you introduce, you deepen your control over your coding environment and enhance the efficiency of your workflow.

Lastly, make it a habit to explore hidden commands specific to the modes you frequently use. Each mode often provides key functionalities tailored to the programming language or format, and discovering these can accelerate your coding effectiveness. Reviewing mode documentation through the command C-h m reveals the features, keybindings, and provided commands that you can harness for your specific coding projects.

In conclusion, advancing your mastery of Emacs through harnessing advanced commands empowers you to engage in coding practices that emphasize efficiency, control, and artistry. By exploring commands, keyboards shortcuts, universal arguments, registers, and collaborative features, you create a seamless and productive environment that allows you to hit the bullseye with each coding session. Infuse your practice with the grace and precision of a Zen archer —navigate the complexities of coding with intention, and let every keystroke resonate with clarity and purpose.

12.2. Mastering Emacs Lisp

Mastering Emacs Lisp is an essential pillar in fully harnessing the capabilities of Emacs, transforming your coding practice into a personalized and efficient experience. Emacs Lisp, a dialect of the Lisp programming language, forms the backbone of Emacs's extensibility and customization, enabling you to tailor your coding environment to suit your unique workflow and preferences. This section will guide you on the path to mastering Emacs Lisp, uncovering its potential to enhance your coding practice while embodying the zen-like principles of simplicity and mindfulness.

To embark on this journey, one must first cultivate a solid understanding of the fundamental concepts of Emacs Lisp. At its core, Emacs Lisp is built upon the idea of symbolic computation, where code can be treated as data. Familiarize yourself with basic syntax, including how to define variables and functions. For example, to define a simple variable, you can use the following command:

```
(setq my-variable "Hello, Emacs Lisp!")
```

This sets the variable my-variable to hold the string "Hello, Emacs Lisp!"—an expression that highlights the straightforward, readable nature of Lisp code. Similarly, defining a simple function can be achieved using:

```
(defun greet ()
  "A simple greeting function."
  (message "Hello from Emacs Lisp!"))
```

Understanding these basic constructs is a critical stepping stone toward more complex integrations and customizations.

As you become comfortable with basic syntax, delve into the collection of built-in functions provided by Emacs Lisp. The extensive library available through Emacs, often referred to as the Emacs Lisp Reference Manual, acts as a valuable resource as you explore functions designed to work seamlessly within the Emacs environment. It is important to reference this manual often, much like a Zen practitioner returns to their teachings for deeper understanding and insight.

One powerful aspect of Emacs Lisp is the ability to manipulate buffers, windows, and frames programmatically. Learning functions that allow you to create, switch, and modify buffers enhances your coding efficiency significantly. Consider the following example that lists all open buffers:

```
(defun list-open-buffers ()
  "Display a list of all open buffers."
  (interactive)
  (buffer-list))
```

By programmatically leveraging these features, your prompts for creating and managing buffers can be tailored to your specific needs. This flexibility creates a customized experience that promotes clarity and focus, resonating with the philosophies of Zen.

Moreover, mastering Emacs Lisp often involves the integration of custom keybindings to enhance your workflow. Through the power of global-set-key, you can bind frequently used functions to specific key combinations, streamlining access to your preferred commands and utilities. For instance, invoking the function you defined for listing buffers could be bound to the key C-c b:

```
(global-set-key (kbd "C-c b") 'list-open-buffers)
```

This powerful command enables you to access functionality with a single keystroke, embodying the efficiency that resonates with Zen principles—the clear and intentional execution of actions with minimal effort.

As you develop your Emacs Lisp skills, consider utilizing the interactive debugging tools provided by the environment. The edebug debugger allows you to step through your code while executing functions, enabling you to inspect variables and program flow. This interaction not only reveals the inner workings of your code but encourages a deeper level of understanding—transforming potential frustrations into insightful learning experiences.

Another valuable technique is to use the use-package macro for managing Emacs packages efficiently. With use-package, you can streamline the configuration of packages, specifying options and setup in a clear and concise way. For instance, using:

```
(use-package magit
  :ensure t
  :bind ("C-x g" . magit-status))
```

This code block ensures that Magit is installed and binds it to `C-x g`, allowing for convenient access. The approach emphasizes the importance of organization and clarity—a principle rooted in both effective coding and Zen practices.

Further, consider the development of custom modes for specific projects or tasks. By defining a major or minor mode tailored to your needs, you enable a seamless alignment between your coding environment and the unique requirements of each project. This practice echoes the Zen philosophy of intent, where each element of your workflow reflects thoughtful consideration of how it serves your goals.

Engaging with the Emacs community can also enrich your journey toward mastering Emacs Lisp. Participate in forums, attend conferences, or contribute to open-source projects that utilize Emacs Lisp. By fostering connections with fellow coders and sharing insights, you cultivate a collaborative spirit that echoes the values of Zen—where community nourishes individual growth.

Lastly, the key to mastering Emacs Lisp lies in continuous practice and exploration. As you experiment with new functions, write and refine your own code, and embrace challenges, allow yourself to grow through the process. Celebrate milestones along the way, reflecting on the progress you've made—from using basic constructs to creating intricate customizations that enhance your coding journey.

In summary, mastering Emacs Lisp is a transformative aspect of your coding practice that embodies intention, clarity, and mindfulness. By understanding the basics, leveraging built-in functions, customizing keybindings, engaging in interactive debugging, utilizing package management techniques, developing custom modes, and embracing community involvement, you pave the way for an enriching experience. Embrace this journey with grace, and let your mastery extend beyond technical proficiency—becoming a testament to the zen-like principles that resonate deeply within your development path. As you continue to explore and expand your skills in Emacs Lisp, may each line of code you write reflect the artistry, focus, and clarity that are the hallmarks of a true coding master.

12.3. Leveraging External Tools

Leveraging external tools is a vital practice in coding that allows developers to extend the capabilities of Emacs, creating a more powerful and personalized coding environment. By integrating external tools into your Emacs setup, you can significantly enhance productivity, streamline workflows, and cultivate a more effective coding practice. Much like a Zen archer who skillfully employs various equipment to achieve precision, integrating the right tools can provide you with the means to hit your coding targets with clarity and efficiency.

To begin with, identifying the external tools that align with your coding workflow is essential. These tools can include various version control systems, build automation software, documentation generators, and even cloud services. Each tool serves a specific purpose and enhances different facets of your development experience. For instance, Git is a widely used version control system that not only helps you manage code changes but also facilitates collaboration among team members. Integrating Git with Emacs through the Magit package streamlines version control operations, allowing you to perform tasks such as committing changes, merging branches, and viewing diffs—all within a user-friendly interface.

Beyond version control, consider build automation tools such as Make or Maven, which orchestrate the process of compiling and packaging your code. Integrating these tools into Emacs allows for seamless execution of build commands directly from your coding environment. By nesting build commands within key bindings or macros, you ensure that project builds can be initiated with minimal disruption, allowing you to maintain your flow and concentration.

When it comes to documentation, tools like Doxygen or Sphinx can significantly enhance code clarity and maintainability. Integrating these documentation generators into your Emacs workflow allows you to document code effectively and generate user-friendly manuals directly from your source code. By establishing documentation as an integral part of your coding practice, you foster clearer communication with collaborators and ensure a smoother onboarding process for new team members.

Cloud services also offer opportunities to integrate external tools into your Emacs setup. For developers working in collaborative environments, services such as GitHub provide an extensive platform for hosting code and managing projects. By integrating GitHub with Emacs, you can facilitate smooth data sharing, issue tracking, and project management directly from your editor. Accessing GitHub through Emacs streamlines workflows, encouraging seamless transitions between coding and collaboration.

To leverage external tools effectively, it is crucial to maintain an adaptable mindset. Just as an archer adjusts their techniques based on varying conditions, coding practices must evolve with the integration of new tools and technologies. This adaptability allows you to continuously refine your workflow, ensuring that external tools enhance rather than complicate your coding processes. Regularly evaluate your toolchain and reflect on how well each tool serves your needs. Be open to experimenting with new tools that emerge, and be willing to phase out those that no longer contribute to your effectiveness.

Incorporating external tools can also foster a sense of community and shared growth. Engaging with online forums, attending workshops, or participating in meetups can uncover novel tools or techniques that colleagues or other developers utilize. Sharing your experiences with tool integrations not only contributes to your community's knowledge base but also strengthens your connections with fellow coders. As with any shared practice, collaborative exploration of external tools encourages innovation and collective learning.

Lastly, take time to document your experiences with integrating external tools into your Emacs environment. Crafting tutorials, writing blog posts, or sharing insights within your coding community ensures the knowledge is retained and can be passed along to others. This mirrors the practice of Zen, where teachings and insights are shared for the benefit of the collective.

In conclusion, leveraging external tools within Emacs enables you to enhance your coding workflow and achieve a more robust coding environment. By integrating version control, build automation, documentation tools, and cloud services, you can streamline your process, enhance collaboration, and foster continuous improvement. Embrace adaptability, engage with your community, and document your learning journey as you integrate these external tools into your practice. As you develop these skills, the clarity and precision of your coding practice will sharpen, much like that of a Zen archer mastering their techniques for the ultimate aim.

12.4. Advanced Debugging Techniques

Advanced Debugging Techniques within Emacs require understanding both the toolset available and the mindset necessary to tackle issues efficiently and effectively. As coding grows in complexity, the need to debug becomes paramount, and leveraging Emacs' capabilities can lead to an agile, refined approach to understanding and resolving errors. This section will guide you through the advanced debugging techniques, emphasizing a combination of tools and strategies that turn frustration into insight, much like a Zen archer recalibrating their stance for precise shooting.

To begin, Emacs maintains a robust suite of built-in debugging features that enhance your coding experience. One of the most valuable tools is the `edebug` mode, an interactive debugger specifically designed for Emacs Lisp. Edebug allows you to step through code execution one line at a time, inspect variable values, and understand function flow in a manner that is both systematic and skillful. Activate it by marking a function with `M-x edebug-defun` or inserting debug traces with `M-x toggle-debug-on-error`. This immediate feedback loop allows you to engage deeply with your code's logical structure, facilitating learning through exploration and hands-on discovery.

Additionally, harness the power of the `debug` feature, which can catch errors and trigger debugging sessions when exceptions occur. By toggling `debug-on-error` with (`setq debug-on-error t`), your Emacs environment will automatically enter debug mode whenever an error is raised. This practice is akin to an archer preparing for any eventualities that may unfold; you remain poised to dive into the issue the moment it presents itself, providing a proactive rather than reactive approach to error handling.

Another remarkable tool to complement your debugging efforts is the `package-debug` mode, which unveils debugging information for installed packages. When errors or unexpected behaviors arise in package functionalities, accessing this debug information allows you to trace problems back to their source, aiding in identifying and resolving concerns effectively. This aligns closely with the Zen mindset of seeking clarity amid confusion.

Beyond utilizing Emacs features, enhancing debugging techniques often involves cultivating a systematic approach to understanding the root cause of issues. Begin by defining the problem statement clearly: What do you expect the code to do, and how does actual behavior differ? Documenting this disparity allows for structured exploratory debugging, similar to an archer analyzing their missed shots to determine what adjustments must be made.

When encountering a bug, employ a technique known as "rubber duck debugging." Speaking your thought process aloud can help you identify logical fallacies or overlooked assumptions within your code. This approach underscores the importance of articulating your understanding of the problem, promoting awareness that often leads to insightful revelations; it's reminiscent of an archer evaluating their form by discussing their stance.

Explore breakpoint management with `gud` (Grand Unified Debugger), which allows you to attach to processes or programs and set breakpoints during execution. Using commands like `M-x gdb` helps to provide visual feedback on the flow of execution, making it easier to observe when and where errors surface in your codebase. The interplay of breakpoints provides an opportunity to analyze code performance and behavior dynamically, shedding light on the root causes of issues that otherwise may remain hidden.

As issues get resolved, maintaining a clear documentation of the debugging process enhances your understanding and builds a repository of learned insights. Creating a personalized debugging log can serve as a reference point for future resolutions, transforming each resolved error into a learning opportunity. By documenting which strategies worked, any specific issues encountered, and how these were solved, you reinforce a culture of continuous improvement synonymous with Zen practices.

Building community connections is another valuable resource during debugging challenges. Engaging with coding forums, Emacs user groups, or team discussions provides a supportive environment to discuss intricate problems or seek advice. Much like an archer might seek camaraderie and support from fellow archers, camaraderie can strengthen you against the frustrations that often accompany debugging.

Finally, the culmination of advanced debugging techniques revolves around acceptance and adaptability. Recognize that errors are an integral part of the coding process—each resolved issue leads to greater mastery and expertise. By adopting a Zen mindset, you can maintain equanimity as you face challenges, embracing the journey as an opportunity for growth and deeper understanding of your craft.

In summary, advanced debugging techniques in Emacs revolve around leveraging built-in tools, cultivating structured problem-solving approaches, engaging in community support, and fostering a reflective mindset. By exploring features like `edebug`, `debug`, and `gud`, alongside systematic techniques like rubber duck debugging and documentation, you can transform the debugging process from a daunting task into a learning experience. Embrace this journey with the composure of a Zen archer, celebrating the growth that arises from each challenge encountered on your path to mastery.

12.5. Optimization for Performance

Optimization for Performance in Emacs is crucial for enhancing your coding experience and productivity. In the realm of coding, speed and efficiency often dictate the quality of your workflow. Just like a Zen archer strives for precision and grace in every shot, optimizing Emacs for performance can significantly streamline your coding process, allowing you to hit your targets with clarity and intention. This section will delve into various strategies, configurations, and plugins that you can leverage to enhance Emacs's performance, ensuring a seamless and focused coding experience.

To begin, it is essential to evaluate your current Emacs configuration. Over time, as you add plugins and customize settings, Emacs can become slow and unresponsive. Conduct a thorough review of your `init.el` or `.emacs` file to identify unnecessary packages, redundant settings, or conflicts that could hinder performance. Removing or disabling these elements allows Emacs to run more smoothly, reminiscent of an archer lightening their load for improved mobility and focus. Aim for a streamlined setup that retains only those packages and configurations that genuinely enhance your coding experience.

One effective way of optimizing performance is to minimize startup time. Emacs can be sluggish during startup if it has to load too many packages or complex configurations. Consider deferring the loading of certain packages until they are needed by using the `use-package` macro. This approach enables you to specify when packages should load, greatly improving the startup speed of Emacs. For example, you can configure `use-package` as follows:

```
(use-package some-package
  :defer t)
```

This ensures that `some-package` only loads when you call it, reducing the overall load time and keeping Emacs responsive from the moment you start it. It's similar to an archer preparing their equipment only when it's time to take aim, allowing for a focused launch.

Next, improve Emacs's performance by taking advantage of lazy loading, which can also be implemented through use-package. Lazy loading helps ensure that packages are only activated when necessary, helping to speed up Emacs further. For example:

```
(use-package some-package
  :commands (some-command)
  :init
  (add-hook 'some-mode-hook 'some-initialization-function))
```

This configuration enables some-package and its associated functions to be loaded only when some-command is executed, enhancing overall response and usability.

Another key optimization involves configuring garbage collection settings, which impacts how efficiently Emacs manages memory resources. By default, Emacs may allocate memory from time to time, leading to potential pauses during your coding sessions. You can adjust this by setting a higher threshold for garbage collection, as shown below:

```
(setq gc-cons-threshold (* 100 1024 1024)) ;; Set to 100 MB
```

Setting the garbage collection threshold this way reduces interruptions and enhances performance, allowing for smoother coding experiences.

Optimizing how Emacs interacts with the file system can also lead to substantial performance improvements. Consider running Emacs with native compilation enabled (if your system supports it) to enhance the speed of elisp execution. This advanced configuration compiles Emacs Lisp files into native code upon loading, resulting in quicker evaluations and responses. You can enable this compilation by configuring your Emacs installation as follows:

```
(setq native-comp-async-jobs-number 4) ;; Adjust based on your CPU cores
```

This configuration allows Emacs to compile in the background while you continue to work, greatly enhancing responsiveness.

Moreover, exploring the use of auto-save options can improve performance significantly. Enabling periodic auto-saving of buffers ensures that your work is preserved without the need for manual saves, allowing you to focus on coding rather than on managing files. Configure auto-save options in your Emacs setup:

```
(setq auto-save-default t)
(setq auto-save-timeout 20) ;; Autosave every 20 seconds
```

By implementing auto-save efficiently, you create an environment where interruptions are minimized, fostering a mindful coding atmosphere that promotes creativity.

Utilize package management effectively. Some plugins can further enhance performance while removing others that may be outdated or unnecessary. A comprehensive way to measure package performance is to utilize the profile command with:

```
M-x elp-instrument-package RET some-package
```

This command allows you to profile the performance of a specific package during usage, evaluating its impact on Emacs's responsiveness. By understanding the performance dynamics of individual packages, you can make informed decisions about retaining, replacing, or refocusing your Emacs setup.

Consider leveraging built-in optimization tools specific to the language mode you regularly utilize. For instance, if you are a web developer, integrated tools like web-mode enhances editing performance compared to the traditional modes, offering context-aware code navigation and formatting features, while remaining lightweight. Each addition should reflect intentionality, as the Zen mindset encourages awareness about both the tools and their implications on your workflow.

Finally, as an essential component of embracing performance optimization, regularly check for updates in both Emacs itself and the packages you utilize. The Emacs development community actively releases updates that often contain performance improvements, bug fixes, and new features that can benefit your Emacs experience. Maintain an active stance towards keeping your environment fresh, allowing you to maximize the advantages of being an Emacs user.

In summary, optimizing Emacs for performance involves a multi-faceted approach focusing on efficient configuration, lazy loading, managing memory effectively, and maintaining your environment up to date. By evaluating your setup critically and adopting best practices rooted in intentionality and mindfulness, you will cultivate a coding experience that resonates with clarity, ease, and productivity. Just as a Zen archer hones their craft through refinement of technique and thoughtful preparation, you can achieve mastery in Emacs optimization, enabling you to hit your coding targets with confidence and precision.

13. Global Perspectives: Zen and Technology

13.1. Zen's Influence on Global Technology Cultures

Zen's Influence on Global Technology Cultures has profoundly reshaped how we think about technology, coding, and collaboration around the world. Emerging from ancient practices centered on mindfulness, simplicity, and harmony, Zen philosophy has permeated various industries, particularly in technology, influencing methodologies, workplace cultures, and even software development itself. This section aims to explore the intersection of Zen philosophy with technological advancements, shedding light on how this wisdom shapes contemporary technology cultures on a global scale.

At its essence, Zen encourages a state of being fully present, fostering awareness and connection to the task at hand. In technology, this translates into reducing distractions and promoting deep work, which is vital in an era increasingly hampered by information overload and constant connectivity. As tech companies began to recognize the role of mindfulness in boosting productivity and creativity, many adopted practices rooted in Zen philosophy. Mindfulness training programs have become common in the workplace, helping employees develop focus, cultivate emotional resilience, and enhance collaboration.

Consider the example of software development methodologies such as Agile and Scrum, which emphasize iterative progress, collaboration, and adaptation. These frameworks echo elements of Zen, embodying principles of simplicity and responsiveness to change—the very essence of being mindful. By breaking projects into manageable tasks and encouraging regular reflection and adaptability, these methodologies promote a Zen-like mindset that embraces uncertainty and fosters the iterative enhancement of work processes.

Furthermore, the integration of mindfulness practices into tech cultures is fostering healthier workplace ecosystems. Mindfulness meditation sessions and quiet spaces for reflection are increasingly common, creating environments conducive to creativity and innovation. Companies like Google and Apple have incorporated mindfulness programs, recognizing that personal well-being translates directly into productivity and more innovative approaches to problem-solving. Here, Zen practices do not merely become a trend; they foster a deeper understanding of the relationship between mental well-being and effective work.

The impact of Zen is also evident in the rise of minimalism within technology design. Many software interfaces and applications have shifted toward cleaner, simpler layouts, reflecting the Zen ideal of simplicity. Design philosophies that prioritize user experience and straightforward navigation are appreciated not only for their aesthetic appeal but also for their functional clarity. This embrace of minimalism is testament to the influence of Zen on how we shape the tools we use, encouraging developers to strip away excess to allow the core functionality to shine.

Case studies illustrate successful integrations of Zen principles into technological innovation. For instance, consider the development of open-source projects that emphasize community contributions, such as Linux or the Apache Software Foundation. These projects are grounded in the principle of mutual support and shared learning —mirroring Zen ideals that stress interconnectedness and collaboration. By fostering inclusive communities where individuals contribute selflessly toward a common goal, these projects exemplify the collective spirit built upon Zenvalues.

Cultivating global tech communities further embodies Zen principles. As the digital landscape becomes increasingly interconnected, diverse voices and perspectives become essential in shaping technological advancements. Emphasizing compassion, empathy, and inclusivity, tech communities work to ensure that technology serves everyone in society equitably. Events such as hackathons, meetups, and collaborative efforts deepen connections among diverse populations, merging different approaches and solutions to address various challenges.

As digital transformation accelerates, the future of technology will continue to reflect the values of Zen. Promoting sustainable and ethical innovations will be at the forefront of discussions around technology's role in society. By infusing mindfulness into product development and ensuring tools contribute positively to well-being, the spirit of Zen will guide the trajectory of technology toward solutions that enhance human life rather than detract from it.

In conclusion, the influence of Zen philosophy on global technology cultures is evidenced by the emphasis on mindfulness, simplicity, and collaboration in professional practices. By integrating Zen principles into coding methodologies and workplace frameworks, technology firms create environments conducive to innovation while nurturing well-being. As we move forward, a conscious and compassionate approach will shape the future of technology, affirming the importance of both the technology we create and the impact it has on our collective human experience. Embrace this influence and allow it to guide you toward a mindful, sustainable future in technology, reflecting the wisdom and values inherent in Zen teachings.

13.2. The Rise of Mindfulness in Tech

The intersection of mindfulness and technology represents a burgeoning conversation within the tech industry, significantly accelerating the integration of mindfulness practices into everyday work environments. As organizations strive to improve productivity while reducing stress and burnout, the principles of mindfulness resonate deeply with professionals, encouraging a balanced approach to work that promotes mental clarity, creativity, and collaboration.

In today's fast-paced world, distractions abound, often leading to a frantic pace of work that can be unsustainable in the long term. Thus, the adoption of mindfulness reflects a desire to slow down, center oneself, and reconnect with the intrinsic purpose of our labor. The emergence of mindfulness programs in various tech companies signifies a growing awareness of the importance of fostering a healthy culture that prioritizes employee well-being alongside business objectives.

Benefits of integrating mindfulness into tech environments are manifold. Employees report enhanced focus, improved emotional regulation, and heightened creativity—all of which can lead to higher-quality work and increased job satisfaction. By practicing mindfulness techniques such as meditation, deep breathing exercises, and reflective pauses, individuals learn to manage stress more effectively, navigate complex challenges with greater ease, and cultivate a deeper sense of presence in their work.

Moreover, mindfulness practices can transform how teams collaborate. Encouraging open communication channels, fostering empathy, and nurturing a culture of inclusivity lead to more effective teamwork. In a supportive environment, team members can share challenges, brainstorm innovative solutions, and celebrate successes together, building a sense of community that echoes the deeper societal impacts tech can have.

As this mindfulness movement continues to rise within tech, it also serves to empower individual professionals on their personal journeys. By learning to integrate mindfulness with their technical skills, software developers can experience profound personal growth, leading them to approach coding—not merely as a series of tasks—but as a creative and fulfilling expression of their identity. Mindfulness helps coders appreciate the artistry inherent in crafting elegant solutions, enriching their professional experience beyond achieving deadlines.

Ultimately, the rise of mindfulness in technology culture underscores our collective yearning for balance and purpose, fostering a holistic approach to work that embraces both the technical and the human. By prioritizing mindfulness, the tech industry can nurture healthier work environments, create more sustainable practices, and empower professionals to thrive—both personally and collectively—in their coding journeys. In doing so, coders can embody the spirit of the Zen archer, aiming for the bullseye of coding excellence with focus, clarity, and grace.

13.3. Case Studies in Zen-Centric Development

In the subchapter titled "Case Studies in Zen-Centric Development," we will delve into practical examples and real-world scenarios where the principles of Zen have been effectively integrated into software development practices, leading to not only enhanced technical proficiency but also a more mindful and purposeful approach to coding. These case studies illustrate how Zen philosophy can shape and enrich the technological landscape, showcasing the seamless blend of artistry and functionality that characterizes successful Zen-centric development.

To begin, let's consider a prominent tech company that implemented Zen principles into its software development cycle. This company recognized that rapid product releases often led to increased stress levels among team members, hampering their creativity and overall productivity. In response, they adopted a more iterative and mindful approach to development by incorporating regular reflection sessions —akin to Zen practices of mindfulness and contemplation. These sessions encouraged developers to share their experiences, discuss challenges they faced, and suggest ways to optimize their coding processes. As a result, the development team not only enhanced their workflows but also fostered a strengthened sense of community, which led to a resurgence in motivation and creativity. This demonstrates that by taking the time to pause and reflect, the company not only improved product quality but also nurtured a positive work environment.

Next, we explore how a small open-source project community utilized Zen principles to enhance collaboration and inclusivity. The project leaders emphasized the importance of clear communication and empathetic engagement among contributors. By adopting a "no blame" culture, where errors and misunderstandings were treated as learning opportunities rather than sources of contention, the community cultivated an atmosphere of patience and respect. Regular check-ins and feedback loops encouraged members to engage openly, allowing for early detection of issues and a collective problem-solving approach.

The result was a vibrant, innovative community whose members felt valued for their contributions—ultimately enhancing the quality of the project and fostering a sense of shared purpose.

In another case study, a software development team embraced Zen practices through the implementation of task management frameworks such as Kanban. By visualizing the flow of work and limiting active tasks, team members could maintain focus while prioritizing quality over speed. This approach led to more thoughtful and intentional development cycles, minimizing stress and reducing the risk of technical debt—an issue that often plagues fast-paced teams. As developers adopted a mindful stance, they found greater satisfaction in their work and a deeper connection to the projects they were cultivating. Here, the principles of Zen—such as simplicity and intentionality—were translated effectively into day-to-day workflows, highlighting how structured yet flexible approaches can lead to success.

The inclusion of mindfulness training as part of onboarding programs at various tech companies represents another powerful case study in Zen-centric development. These organizations recognized that fostering a culture of mindfulness in the workplace can lead to improved mental health and well-being among employees. New hires were introduced to basic mindfulness techniques, such as breath awareness and reflective practices, promoting a calm and focused atmosphere from the start. As mindfulness became an integral part of the company culture, team members experienced heightened emotional endurance during challenging projects, leading to improved collaboration and communication amidst stress. This integration of Zen principles reflects a holistic understanding of the workforce, where mental well-being is prioritized alongside productivity.

Additionally, innovative coding boot camps have begun to weave Zen principles into their curricula, training aspiring developers in both technical skills and mindful coding practices. By emphasizing the value of patience, self-reflection, and empathy, these programs prepare students to approach coding not just as a set of technical tasks but as an opportunity for creative expression and personal growth.

Students are encouraged to engage in collaborative projects, where mutual support and feedback are core tenets. This approach fosters a sense of community that mirrors the interdependent relationships central to Zen practice, promoting both technical skills and personal development in a supportive environment.

Lastly, we can look to the lessons learned from companies that have integrated agile methodologies, emphasizing adaptability while maintaining a foundation in Zen principles. Agile emphasizes responsiveness to change while remaining aligned with user needs, paving the way for high-quality deliverables without compromising on developer well-being. This approach embodies Zen's fluidity—allowing teams to pivot quickly while grounding decision-making in mindfulness, collaboration, and self-awareness.

In conclusion, the case studies surrounding Zen-centric development illustrate the powerful impact that Zen principles can have on software development practices. By incorporating mindfulness, reflection, and holistic approaches into their workflows, tech companies and communities have witnessed significant improvements in collaboration, productivity, and overall job satisfaction. Ultimately, these examples highlight the art of coding as a journey of self-discovery and creativity—an endeavor where the principles of Zen serve as guiding lights, illuminating the path toward mastery and fulfillment in the technological landscape.

13.4. Cultivating Global Tech Communities

Cultivating global tech communities is a vital pursuit that contributes significantly to the development of innovative ideas, diverse perspectives, and ethical technologies in the software development landscape. In an interconnected world, the opportunity to foster understanding and collaboration across boundaries creates a rich tapestry of shared knowledge, affirming the essential role that inclusive tech communities play in shaping the future of technology.

At the heart of cultivating global tech communities lies the recognition of the value of diversity. Diverse communities—the cultural, ethnic, and gender variety found within them—bring unique viewpoints and experiences that can inspire creativity and spur innovation. Embracing this diversity fosters an environment where various ideas intersect, leading to more holistic solutions that address the multi-faceted challenges present in today's tech landscape. By encouraging diverse voices to participate in discussions, projects, and decision-making processes, we create a dynamic environment where everyone feels empowered to contribute.

One key aspect of developing these communities is intentionally creating spaces that welcome and support underrepresented groups in tech. This might involve initiatives such as mentorship programs, coding boot camps, or networking events designed to bridge gaps in representation. Creating such opportunities helps ensure that marginalized voices have a seat at the table, enriching the community while cultivating a sense of belonging. Just as Zen philosophy emphasizes inclusivity and interconnectedness, tech communities should reflect these principles, creating safe and supportive environments for all.

Moreover, global tech communities can lean on technology tools that facilitate collaboration across time zones and geographical boundaries. Platforms such as GitHub, Slack, and other project management tools allow developers from around the world to share ideas, contribute to projects, and support one another in real-time. By leveraging these tools, coding communities can transcend physical barriers, fostering collaboration and ensuring that innovation flourishes regardless of location.

As communities evolve and grow, prioritizing communication and transparency is paramount. Clear guidelines regarding collaboration protocols, expectations, and feedback mechanisms can significantly enhance members' experiences and promote a culture of constructive engagement. Embracing open-source methodologies can facilitate efficient collaboration, allowing developers to contribute to larger projects while reaping the benefits of collective insights and expertise.

In addition to technical collaboration, fostering connections amongst community members is essential for building a supportive environment. Hosting events such as hackathons, workshops, and meetups provides opportunities for face-to-face interactions, allowing individuals to form bonds that deepen their relationships. Establishing mentorship programs, where experienced developers guide novices through challenges, strengthens ties and promotes knowledge transfer—ensuring that learning flows freely within the community.

Furthermore, cultivating a mindset grounded in empathy can enrich community dynamics. Encouraging members to actively and compassionately engage with one another cultivates awareness of individual needs and fosters collaboration. Implementing practices such as peer reviews not only improves code quality but encourages discussion, reflection, and mutual understanding. When team members treat one another with respect and compassion, it reflects the values inherent in Zen traditions— laying the groundwork for communities where innovation can thrive.

Ultimately, as tech communities spring up around the globe, they must remain rooted in the principles of sustainability and ethical responsibility. Collaboration should not only aim for innovation but also prioritize the societal impact of technology. Advocacy for ethical coding practices, equitable access to resources, and a commitment to positively contributing to the greater good are fundamental. By embedding these values into the community's culture, we pave the way for technology that serves humanity and promotes well-being.

In conclusion, cultivating global tech communities brings about opportunities for diversity, creativity, empathy, and ethical innovation in the digital landscape. By embracing the ideals of inclusion and collaboration, tech communities foster an environment where ideas thrive, problems are tackled collectively, and individuals feel empowered. Through engagement, open communication, mentorship, and a commitment to social responsibility, upward trends in innovation will emerge. This journey embodies the essence of Zen—where every connection, idea, and initiative is seen as threads contributing to a greater tapestry of understanding and progress in the tech world. By harnessing these collective efforts, we enable a future where technology is developed through shared wisdom, compassion, and innovation.

13.5. Building a Zen Future in Technology

Building a Zen future in technology hinges on the integration of mindfulness, intentionality, and compassion into our coding practices and the broader tech landscape. As technology continues to evolve at an unprecedented pace, the quest for a harmonious approach to development becomes ever more critical. By drawing upon principles from Zen philosophy and embracing them within our professional conduct, we can nurture advancements that not only fulfill technical needs but also resonate positively with the human experience, setting the stage for a future where technology serves the greater good.

At the core of creating a Zen-inspired tech future is the concept of mindfulness in coding. Mindfulness allows coders to engage deeply with their work, fostering a sense of focus and presence that enhances creativity and problem-solving. When we approach coding with an attitude of mindfulness, we learn to appreciate the artistry inherent in our craft, recognizing that every line of code is an expression of intention and thoughtfulness. This mindfulness can be cultivated through regular reflection on our practices, promoting a growth mindset that values progress over perfection and encourages us to embrace the learning journey through challenges.

Moreover, the choice of tools and technologies we adopt plays a significant role in shaping a Zen future. Embracing open-source technologies and collaborative frameworks facilitates a more inclusive approach to coding that aligns with Zen principles of compassion and interconnectedness. By cultivating a supportive coding community, where knowledge and resources are shared generously, we contribute to an ecosystem that fosters innovation while ensuring everyone benefits from collective advancements. This spirit of collaboration echoes the teachings of Zen—where the journey is not undertaken alone, but rather through a web of connections that enriches our shared experiences.

Another critical aspect of building a Zen future in technology is the commitment to ethical practices. As technology continues to proliferate, it is our responsibility as coders to ensure that our innovations honor the values of respect, empathy, and sustainability. Adopting practices such as inclusive design, user-centered development, and data privacy aligns our work with the greater good, ensuring our technology enhances lives rather than diminishes them. This commitment transcends technical boundaries and invites us to consider the broader implications of our work, creating solutions that resonate positively within society.

Furthermore, embracing the principles of simplicity and clarity in design enhances the user experience, mirroring the Zen ideal of minimalism. As we cultivate solutions that are intuitive and easy to navigate, we promote a sense of calm within the digital experience. This focus on simplicity fosters a culture of efficiency, allowing users to engage deeply with technology without the unnecessary complexity that often hinders productivity. Additionally, streamlined coding practices contribute to maintainable, scalable codebases, enhancing long-term success and reducing cognitive load for developers.

As we forge ahead, nurturing a culture of lifelong learning becomes a cornerstone for shaping a prosperous tech future. Just as Zen encourages there to be no end to the pursuit of knowledge, we must remain open to new ideas, technologies, and methodologies. Embracing a philosophy of continual growth empowers developers to adapt amidst changing landscapes, ensuring we don't become stagnant in our practices. Investments in training, mentorship, and knowledge-sharing initiatives within teams sustain this commitment to learning, allowing us to collectively develop our skills and understanding.

Ultimately, building a Zen future in technology requires a commitment to a holistic approach that intertwines mindfulness, collaboration, ethical practices, simplicity, and lifelong learning. As coders, we possess the remarkable ability to shape the new digital world through our actions and decisions, ensuring technology serves humanity and enhances our experience. Let us embrace the teachings of Zen, drawing inspiration from the principles we've explored, as we work toward a future where technology resonates harmoniously with the human spirit, creating a landscape filled with empathy, creativity, and collective success.

14. The Spiritual Journey of a Zen Coder

14.1. The Internal Landscape of Zen Coding

The Internal Landscape of Zen Coding

The journey into the internal landscape of Zen coding unveils a unique interplay between technology and mindfulness, where the coder's state of mind can significantly influence their coding practice and overall satisfaction. Much like the meditative state a Zen archer achieves before releasing their arrow, the internal landscape for coders is deeply intertwined with their mental clarity, emotional balance, and consciousness during the act of coding. This section explores various aspects that shape this internal terrain, providing insights into how coders can cultivate mindfulness, reflection, and intentionality within their coding practices.

At the heart of Zen coding is the principle of mindfulness—being fully present and engaged in the moment without distraction. This practice encourages coders to embrace each line of code as a reflection of their intentions, allowing them to connect deeply with the work they create. When mindfulness is woven into the fabric of coding, it creates an environment where focus flourishes, mistakes can be viewed as learning opportunities, and creativity blossoms. Coders can achieve this state by establishing rituals that signal the transition into a mindful mode of coding. For instance, taking a few moments of quiet reflection before launching into a coding session can set the tone for deeper engagement with the work.

The environment in which one codes also plays a critical role in shaping this internal landscape. A cluttered workspace filled with distractions can lead to a chaotic mindset, hindering focus and creativity. Conversely, a clean and organized environment facilitates clarity and calmness, encouraging individuals to immerse themselves in their coding tasks fully. Coders can enhance their physical space through simple actions such as decluttering their desks, ensuring optimal lighting, and minimizing digital distractions. By creating a serene coding environment, the coder can cultivate an internal land-scape that mirrors their external surroundings.

Additionally, the practice of journaling is a valuable tool for fostering reflection and deepening understanding of one's coding journey. Recording thoughts, emotions, and experiences related to coding en-courages self-awareness—a key aspect of Zen philosophy. Coders can reflect on what went well, what challenges they faced, and how they responded to stressors. This practice allows for insight into personal growth and development, helping to navigate future coding endeav-ors with greater confidence and resilience. Journaling reinforces the understanding that the coding landscape is not only about the lines of code but also the emotional and mental terrain that accompanies each project.

Another aspect of the internal landscape of Zen coding involves embracing imperfection and accepting that mistakes are part of the learning process. Just as a Zen archer does not strive for infallibility with every shot but rather learns from missed targets, coders need to cultivate a mindset that values adaptability and growth. When confronted with bugs or errors, embrace them with curiosity instead of frustration. Analyzing these moments fosters resilience; each bug resolved becomes a stepping stone toward mastery.

Regularly practicing gratitude is also integral to enriching the internal landscape of Zen coding. Take time to appreciate the small victories accomplished during coding sessions, whether it be successfully im-plementing a challenging feature or making progress toward a long-term project. By acknowledging these achievements and expressing gratitude for the opportunity to create, coders can reinforce a positive mindset that nurtures motivation and creativity. A grateful attitude enables a deeper connection to the work, allowing for a fuller expe-rience of joy and intentionality in coding.

Sensory engagement is another dimension in which one can cultivate a Zen coding practice. Allow the sensory experience of coding—the keystrokes, the rhythm of typing, the unfolding of ideas—to become intertwined with your awareness. Practicing mindfulness through tactile engagement can deepen concentration and enhance the feeling of presence as you work. Engaging fully in the physical aspects of coding fosters a more conscious connection to the written code, amplifying the experience of creation.

The final consideration within this internal landscape revolves around community. Engaging with like-minded individuals fosters collective growth while encouraging sharing experiences, insights, and techniques. Participate in coding workshops, online forums, or open-source projects that resonate with your interests. The sense of connection to a community that embodies Zen values can amplify your coding journey, offering support and encouragement along the way. This interconnectedness speaks to the principle of compassion and empathy, core tenets of both Zen practice and collaborative coding.

In conclusion, the internal landscape of Zen coding is cultivated through mindfulness, reflection, and intention. By creating an environment that promotes clarity, engaging in reflective practices like journaling, embracing imperfection, practicing gratitude, nurturing sensory engagement, and fostering community, coders can enrich their internal journey. As one learns to navigate their emotional and mental terrain, the experience of coding transforms into a rewarding practice that resonates with purpose and artistry—a precious intersection of technology and Zen. Embarking on this path encourages each coder to develop not only technical skills but also emotional intelligence, leading them toward greater mastery and fulfillment in their craft. Each keystroke, resonating with intention and clarity, becomes a reflection of the Zen journey, where coding is both an art and a mindful practice.

14.2. Transcending Technical Boundaries

Transcending technical boundaries involves embracing a mindset where creativity, adaptability, and the principles of design and clarity become as essential as technical proficiency itself. In the fast-paced world of coding, developers often find themselves faced with challenges that seem insurmountable or constrained by the limitations of technology. However, like the Zen archer who transcends their limitations through focus and intention, programmers too can learn to rise above technical barriers and approach problems with innovative solutions.

At the core of transcending these boundaries lies the ability to think outside of traditional frameworks. Encouraging creative problem-solving techniques allows coders to explore new methodologies and embrace unconventional paths when faced with obstacles. This shifts the focus from being confined by existing methods to recognizing that solutions can exist outside typical patterns. Engaging in brainstorming sessions or collaborative coding practices brings a diversity of perspectives into problem-solving, enabling teams to harness collective genius to overcome technical hurdles.

Emphasizing a design-thinking approach can also play a critical role in transcending technical restrictions. Design thinking encourages an iterative process of empathizing with users, defining problems, ideating solutions, prototyping, and testing. By reframing technical challenges as design problems, coders can approach their work with a mindset open to exploring various solutions and adaptations. Much like the Zen archer evaluates factors—distance, wind, and trajectory —during practice, coding challenges become opportunities for design exploration instead of rigid, linear processes confined to conventional programming practices.

Fostering an environment that embraces experimentation can also lead to groundbreaking solutions. When teams feel psychologically safe to try new ideas and embrace failure as part of the learning process, breakthroughs are often on the horizon. This courage to pursue innovative avenues starkly resembles how skilled archers adapt and refine their techniques through relentless practice and experimentation.

Equally important is the practice of continuous learning. In a rapidly evolving technological landscape, the skills and frameworks that worked effectively yesterday may not necessarily apply tomorrow. Cultivating a mindset that embraces lifelong learning empowers coders to stay ahead of trends, adapt to advancements, and explore languages and frameworks that complement their current skill sets. Attending workshops, participating in coding boot camps, or joining user groups dedicated to specific technologies can enhance understanding and performance—ensuring that technical boundaries are not seen as immovable constraints but rather as opportunities for growth.

In addition, building bridges between disciplines can also facilitate transcending technical limitations. Embracing an interdisciplinary mindset encourages developers to draw inspiration from fields such as design, psychology, or sociology to inform their coding practices and enhance user experience. This cross-pollination of ideas sparks creativity and innovation, allowing for richer, more meaningful solutions that address user needs effectively.

Moreover, the focus on sustainable coding practices paves the way for transcending technical boundaries. By emphasizing clean code, clear documentation, and adherence to coding standards, developers create a codebase that is easier to maintain, adapt, and evolve over time. This means that when new technologies emerge or project requirements shift, the foundation built on sustainable practices is resilient enough to accommodate these changes without significant friction.

Finally, fostering a compassionate perspective toward users and the coding community at large can lead to user-centric solutions and enrich the coding journey. Understanding user needs prompts coders to view their work as an extension of humanity, encouraging a focus on ethical implications and greater responsibilities—ensuring that technology is designed to serve all stakeholders with respect and empathy.

In conclusion, transcending technical boundaries involves embracing creativity, adaptability, design thinking, and a commitment to lifelong learning. By cultivating an environment that supports experimentation, interdisciplinary engagement, sustainable practices, and compassion, coders can rise above technical limitations and create solutions that resonate with users. Much like the Zen archer who learns to flow seamlessly from one challenge to the next, coders too can embrace this journey—transforming obstacles into opportunities with focus and intention as they navigate the complexities of their craft. Embrace the boundless possibilities that arise from transcending technical confines, and let your coding journey reflect the artistry and mastery inherent in this transformative practice.

14.3. The Zen Path to Code Simplicity

The exploration of the Zen Path to Code Simplicity invites coders to embrace a mindset and practice that encourages clarity, focus, and intentionality in their coding endeavors. The pursuit of simplicity in coding transcends the mere act of writing functional code; it embodies a holistic approach that emphasizes elegance, maintainability, and mindfulness. Like the Zen archer who meticulously refines their aim, coders who prioritize simplicity can significantly enhance their productivity and creativity.

To cultivate simplicity, start by understanding the core concept of minimalism in coding. Minimalism advocates for removing unnecessary complexity, which can obscure understanding and hinder effective collaboration. Simple code is not only easier to read and maintain but also allows for quicker debugging and adaptability. The principle can be embodied by the practice of writing clean code—utilizing meaningful variable names, avoiding overly convoluted logic, and implementing concise functions that serve a single purpose. This reflects the Zen ideal of clarity, where each line of code holds weight and significance.

When approaching a coding problem, take the time to break it down into its elementary components. Instead of attempting to solve a complex problem in one go, deconstruct the issue to identify smaller, manageable parts. This incremental approach allows you to focus on one element at a time, which can lead to clearer thinking and more effective problem-solving. Each small solution can serve as a building block toward a more comprehensive resolution, reminiscent of the Zen practice of focusing on the essence of each moment.

As you engage with Emacs, leverage its configuration capabilities to enhance simplicity in your coding workflow. Streamline your setup by only utilizing the packages and configurations that genuinely improve your experience. Regularly review installed plugins and eliminate those that are no longer necessary; a clutter-free coding environment fosters simplicity and clarity, allowing you to focus solely on the task at hand.

Adopting consistent coding standards within your team also promotes simplicity and cohesion in collaborative projects. Establish common practices that everyone adheres to, such as naming conventions and code formatting requirements. This consistency reduces friction when reviewing code, as developers can quickly understand the logic and purpose behind each implementation. When all members share common standards, the codebase becomes more navigable and welcoming, fostering collaboration and mutual understanding.

To further deepen your commitment to simplicity, embrace iterative and incremental development practices. Continuous integration and deployment (CI/CD) processes allow for small, incremental changes to be tested and deployed. This approach encourages regular reflections on new features and their contributions to the overall project. Zen principles emphasize the importance of ongoing progress, and iterative development embodies this concept, allowing for the benefits of simplicity to manifest in the results produced.

Reflection plays a pivotal role in facilitating simplicity in your coding practice. After completing a project or a significant feature, take the time to review not only your final product but also the process you employed. What went well, and what could have been simplified further? Document these reflections to inform future projects, nurturing an ongoing commitment to simplicity and clarity in your work.

When encountering complex coding challenges, harness the concept of "rubber duck debugging." Explain your problem out loud, as though you were teaching a rubber duck—or even another coder. This intuitive practice helps to crystallize your understanding of the issue at hand, often revealing straightforward solutions amid complexities. Embracing simplicity in the debugging process allows you to approach challenges calmly and creatively, mirroring the Zen principle of ease amidst complexity.

Finally, foster a culture of empathy and support within your coding community. As you pursue simplicity in your coding endeavors, cultivate an environment where team members feel comfortable sharing their struggles and seeking assistance. Encourage conversations around clean and simple coding practices, celebrating the clarity that arises from collective reflection. Just as a Zen community thrives on mutual understanding and compassion, so too can a coding team benefit from shared experiences and support.

In conclusion, the Zen Path to Code Simplicity is a commitment to cultivating clarity, intention, and elegance in your coding practice. By prioritizing minimalism, embracing incremental solutions, fostering consistency, engaging in reflective practices, and nurturing a culture of empathy, you can create a mindful coding environment that enhances productivity and creativity. The simplicity you cultivate within your coding endeavors not only enriches the quality of your work but also aligns with the Zen ideals of harmony and connection. As you navigate this journey toward simplicity, let each line of code reflect clarity and purpose, harmonizing your technical prowess with the essence of Zen.

14.4. The Role of Compassion in Coding

In "The Zen Archer's Emacs: Hit the Bullseye with Each Coding Shot," the notion of compassion in coding extends beyond technical skills to encompass how we interact with ourselves, our code, and others in the programming community. This chapter delves into the profound impact that compassion—rooted deeply in Zen principles—can have on our coding practices, shaping our approach to technology in ways that resonate with empathy, understanding, and respect.

To begin with, compassion in coding involves fostering a mindset that promotes empathy towards users. As developers, we often create software that will be utilized by diverse audiences with varying backgrounds and needs. By adopting a compassionate approach, we prioritize user experience and accessibility, ensuring that our work serves humanity effectively. This practice mirrors the Zen principle that encourages us to consider the impact of our actions on others before proceeding. Taking the time to understand our users' perspectives can significantly enhance the design and functionality of our applications, ultimately leading to technology that resonates on a human level.

Moreover, compassionate coding practices extend to our engagement with teammates and peers. In collaborative environments, misunderstandings, challenges, and diverse perspectives are commonplace. Cultivating compassion within these interactions fosters a supportive atmosphere where team members feel valued and heard. When offering feedback, approach discussions with empathy, framing critiques as opportunities for improvement rather than pointing out shortcomings. This mindset encourages open dialogue and nurtures healthy relationships—essential components of a cohesive and productive coding team. Just as a Zen archer may help fellow practitioners refine their techniques, developers can uplift one another through kind and constructive communication.

The coding community at large can benefit from compassion as well. Embracing a culture of inclusivity is crucial, making space for diverse voices that contribute to the richness of technology. Showcasing solidarity with marginalized groups within the tech industry cultivates a community where everyone feels welcome and empowered to contribute. For instance, supporting initiatives that provide free coding resources, mentorship for underrepresented demographics, or scholarships for coding boot camps exemplifies a compassionate approach to community engagement. By working together, the tech community can break down barriers, promote equity, and foster innovation driven by diverse perspectives and experiences.

Furthermore, compassion also extends to ourselves. It is essential to practice self-compassion as we navigate the complexities of coding. The journey is often fraught with challenges, self-doubt, and the tumult of fast-paced deadlines. Recognizing that mistakes are part of the learning process allows us to step back and adjust our mindset. Instead of criticizing ourselves when facing setbacks, we can view them as valuable learning experiences that contribute to our growth. Embracing self-compassion fosters resilience and reinforces our commitment to continuous improvement—transforming obstacles into opportunities for introspection and development.

Incorporating mindfulness into our coding practices can amplify the role of compassion in our work. Engaging in regular pauses before, during, and after coding sessions provides moments for reflection, gratitude, and awareness of our impact on both our code and those around us. Mindful coding encourages us to be present, maintain focus, and approach each task with compassion and intention—ensuring that our work resonates deeply with ourselves and others.

In conclusion, the role of compassion in coding is a vital principle rooted in Zen philosophy. By fostering empathy towards users, cultivating supportive relationships within teams, investing in our community, embracing self-compassion, and incorporating mindfulness into our coding practices, we create technology that not only serves technical needs but profoundly enriches the human experience. This compassionate approach enhances our coding journey, allowing us to cultivate a mindful practice that resonates with the essence of Zen, ultimately leading us to hit the coding bullseye with intention and grace. As we embrace these principles, we transform our interactions and creations into a shared journey of understanding, innovation, and genuine connection.

14.5. A Lifelong Commitment to Learning

A commitment to lifelong learning is a cornerstone of growth not just in coding, but across all disciplines. It embodies the essence of Zen philosophy, which teaches us to remain open to new experiences, insights, and transformations. In the journey through "The

Zen Archer's Emacs: Hit the Bullseye with Each Coding Shot," this commitment manifests as the desire to integrate Zen principles into every coding practice, continually refining our skills while nurturing our personal development. This section will explore the importance of engaging in lifelong learning and how it can guide you toward mastery in your coding journey.

First and foremost, accepting that coding, like any art or discipline, is an ever-evolving practice is essential. Technologies, programming languages, frameworks, and methodologies frequently change. Embracing a mindset focused on continual learning encourages adaptability, allowing you to transition smoothly between advancements and maintain your relevance within the industry. By understanding that mastery does not end with one's current skill set, you gain the motivation to explore new concepts, embrace diverse technologies, and refine existing practices. This notion aligns with the Zen principle of impermanence, where each moment is an opportunity for growth and redefinition.

Making a conscious effort to expand your knowledge will also furnish you with the tools necessary for improvement. Set specific, achievable learning goals, as these intentions provide a clear direction for your journey. For instance, committing to mastering a new programming language within a specified timeframe, or exploring the latest features of Emacs, enables you to map out your learning path and engage with the material intentionally. Reflecting upon the coding challenges you encounter, seeking resources, and documenting your insights in a structured manner will enhance your understanding and foster mastery.

Participating in coding communities and discussions can significantly enhance your journey. Engaging with like-minded individuals who share your passion for coding can lead to a significant exchange of knowledge, challenges, and support. Contributing to open-source projects, attending meetups, or even joining online forums can provide rich opportunities to learn from others while offering your insights in return. Each interaction within these communities can enrich your understanding and expand your perspective, paralleling the Zen practice of communal support and understanding.

Additionally, teaching and mentoring others can be an extraordinary avenue for your own learning. As you share your knowledge, skills, and insights with less experienced coders, you reinforce your own understanding. It's said that teaching is one of the most effective ways to learn; as you articulate concepts and guide others, you deepen your mastery and uncover gaps in your knowledge. The practice of teaching embodies the Zen ideals of fostering growth in oneself while nurturing the growth of others.

Embracing self-reflection throughout your coding journey is vital—take the time to assess what you've learned, how you've grown, and where you seek to go next. At the end of each project or coding session, reflect on the successes and challenges you've encountered. Analyze your coding choices, thought processes, and responses, and consider how these insights can inform your future work. This reflective practice will not only enhance your coding skills but can also contribute to your personal development.

Moreover, setting aside time for continuous exploration allows you to stay ahead in the ever-changing technology landscape. Dedicate a portion of your weekly or monthly schedule specifically for learning, whether that be through online courses, tutorials, or hands-on projects. This integration of consistent learning opportunities integrates smoothly into your coding routine, ensuring that you remain engaged and curious.

Lastly, never lose sight of the joy of coding itself. The intrinsic motivation behind your craft can fuel your commitment to lifelong learning. Approach coding as both a challenge and an opportunity for creativity—celebrate your successes, big or small, and continue to cultivate enthusiasm for the journey ahead. By embracing the journey of lifelong learning, you live in alignment with the Zen practice of mindfulness and intentionality, always engaging in growth with an open heart and open mind.

In conclusion, a lifelong commitment to learning is an essential element in your journey as a coder. By embodying the principles of Zen—mindfulness, adaptability, and self-reflection—you can remain focused on continuous improvement and growth. Embrace every challenge, seek new opportunities for exploration, and recognize the potential for transformation that exists within each moment. As you navigate your coding journey, allow this commitment to guide you toward mastery and fulfillment, ensuring you hit your coding targets with clarity and purpose.

15. Reflections on The Zen Archer's Emacs

15.1. Revisiting the Connection Between Zen and Emacs

Revisiting the Connection Between Zen and Emacs allows us to reflect on the transformative journey we've undertaken through the pages of this book. The essential principles of Zen—mindfulness, simplicity, clarity, and compassion—have provided a framework for understanding not only how to code efficiently in Emacs but also how to engage with the coding process as a holistic practice. This connection highlights the beauty inherent in the code we write, transforming each line into a purposeful expression of our intentions, rather than merely a technical requirement to fulfill.

In the exploration of Zen and Emacs, we've established that mindfulness in coding enhances focus and presence. The act of consciously engaging with every keystroke and decision fuels creativity and clarity in the problem-solving process. In an age where distractions abound, committing to being present in our coding endeavors fosters a sense of purpose that profoundly impacts the quality of our work. Just like the Zen archer remains attuned to their breathing and surroundings, embracing a mindful approach to coding cultivates a deep connection between coder and craft.

Moreover, the integration of simplicity underscores the value of elegant coding practices. By stripping away unnecessary complexity, we not only produce cleaner, more maintainable code but also engender a deeper understanding of the issues at hand. The metaphor of the Zen archer, who emphasizes ease and grace in their movements, serves as a compelling reminder that coding too can embody simplicity—transforming it into an art rather than a mere technical exercise.

Compassion, both toward users and within team dynamics, takes center stage in this discourse. Prioritizing empathy while designing software ensures that our work positively impacts those who interact with it. By acting with compassion in our coding communities, we create environments that are inclusive and supportive, allowing diverse perspectives to enrich the landscape of technology. The shared journey towards collective mastery reflects the Zen belief in interconnectedness, where our efforts contribute to a greater good.

The lessons learned from this exploration extend beyond technical knowledge; they emphasize the value of personal growth and self-reflection. By instilling mindfulness practices, a commitment to continuous learning, and a willingness to embrace change with grace, we pave the path for ongoing evolution in our coding practices. The Zen archer's wisdom reminds us to embrace our journey, valuing each experience as a catalyst for growth, rather than merely a stepping stone towards achievement.

Crafting a personal Zen coding philosophy entails weaving together these principles with our unique experiences and aspirations as developers. Each coder's journey is distinct, shaped by individual perspectives and challenges. By embracing the insights gained throughout this book, you can define a philosophy that resonates with your values, combining technical proficiency with mindfulness and compassion. This philosophy can evolve over time, reflecting your growth as a coder and aligning with the changing landscape of technology.

Preparing for future coding journeys means taking proactive steps to apply these principles to the challenges and opportunities that lie ahead. Embrace your newfound awareness of mindfulness, simplicity, and compassion as you encounter project deadlines, coding crises, or groundbreaking new technologies. These principles will serve as guiding lights, enabling you to navigate the complexities of coding with clarity and purpose. Embrace a mindset focused on ongoing reflection and adaptation, as these qualities will become essential as you continue along your path toward mastery.

Finally, let us celebrate the achievements made possible by embracing the Zen archer's path. Recognize the progress you've made as you've delved into the intricacies of Emacs and coding, and cherish the insights that will guide your future endeavors. Celebrate not only the completion of projects but also the positive relationships you've developed, the growth in your technical skills, and the mindfulness practices that have complemented your coding journey. This celebration affirms that the path to mastery is not simply about reaching destinations; it is about appreciating the beauty and richness of each moment along the way.

In conclusion, the connection between Zen and Emacs catalyzes a transformative journey into coding that embodies mindfulness, simplicity, compassion, and reflection. By integrating these principles into our work, we unlock the potential for deeper engagement, creative expression, and personal growth. As you move forward, carry these insights with you, nurturing the Zen coding philosophy as an enduring companion in your journey as a developer—the unending path toward mastery awaits, and it's illuminated by your commitment to this practice.

15.2. Lessons Learned from the Zen Archer

Lessons Learned from the Zen Archer provides a comprehensive reflection on the principles and practices that have emerged throughout the journey of blending Zen insights with coding techniques. These lessons distill key takeaways that will serve as invaluable tools for continued personal and professional growth in the coding landscape. Embracing the spirit of the Zen Archer—where each keystroke resembles a carefully released arrow—cultivates a more intentional, focused, and harmonious approach to coding.

1. Mindfulness in Coding: The importance of being present and engaged with your work cannot be overstated. Mindfulness allows for deeper focus and creativity, enabling coders to engage fully with the problems at hand, ultimately producing higher quality code. Practicing mindfulness techniques can enhance your coding sessions, leading to greater insight and innovation.

2. Simplicity and Clarity: Striving for simplicity in code design embodies the Zen principle of minimalism—creating clean, maintainable code that communicates its purpose effectively. The more

concise and clear your code, the easier it is for others to understand and collaborate on, promoting a culture of learning and sharing.

3. Compassion Toward Users and Colleagues: Approaching software development with empathy fosters a user-centric mindset, ensuring that the tools and software we create resonate positively with users. Likewise, compassion within teams nurtures a supportive environment where members feel valued, respected, and empowered to share their thoughts and contributions.

4. Reflective Practice: Regular self-reflection following projects promotes growth and insight. Evaluating one's coding decisions, the challenges faced, and the successes achieved allows for a deeper understanding of one's development journey, reinforcing intentions for future coding endeavors.

5. Community and Collaboration: Engaging with the coding community enriches the learning experience, offering opportunities for knowledge sharing and support. Emphasizing collaboration over individual achievement helps create a positive culture that leads to innovation and collective success.

6. Adaptability to Change: Embracing change as an opportunity for growth is vital in the tech landscape. Adopting a flexible mindset allows coders to navigate new technologies, project requirements, and coding paradigms with grace, enhancing their resilience and adaptability.

7. Embracing the Creative Process: Coding is an art form that involves creativity and expression. Recognizing this aspect encourages a deeper connection to one's work, making the coding journey more fulfilling and enjoyable. By allowing for exploration and experimentation, coders can discover innovative solutions to complex challenges.

8. Commitment to Lifelong Learning: The journey of a coder is one of continuous growth. Embracing a mindset of curiosity, regular practice, and educational opportunities ensures that individuals

remain engaged and skilled in their craft, ready to tackle new challenges as they arise.

Crafting Your Personal Zen Coding Philosophy involves synthesizing these lessons into a guiding framework for your coding journey. Begin by reflecting on your values and aspirations as a coder. How do you want to approach your work? What principles align with your vision for success? Your philosophy can incorporate mindfulness practices, commitments to empathy, continuous learning, and the pursuit of simplicity. Document this philosophy in a visible place—perhaps as a living document in your Emacs configuration or as a visual reminder in your workspace.

Preparing for Future Coding Journeys will require you to keep these Zen lessons close to heart. As you embark on new projects or find yourself faced with unexpected challenges, remind yourself of the principles you've cultivated. Continually engage in mindfulness, embrace simplicity, and foster compassion. Approach each coding endeavor with a mindset focused on growth rather than perfection, and be open to learning from each experience.

Lastly, celebrating your achievements is critical to reinforcing a positive coding journey. Recognize both the large milestones and the small victories along the way. Whether completing a challenging project, learning a new technique, or collaborating effectively with your team, take the time to acknowledge and celebrate your accomplishments. This practice breeds motivation, highlights your growth, and fosters a sense of fulfillment in your coding journey.

By internalizing these lessons and principles, you set the stage for continued success, enabling you to navigate the ever-changing landscape of coding with the calm focus of a Zen archer—ready to hit the bullseye with every keystroke. Embrace this journey, and allow it to illuminate your path toward mastery in your craft.

15.3. Crafting Your Personal Zen Coding Philosophy

Crafting Your Personal Zen Coding Philosophy invites coders to take the rich insights gained throughout this journey and integrate them into a cohesive framework that shapes individual coding practices. Just as a Zen archer draws upon essential principles to refine their technique and enhance their performance, coders can develop a philosophy that harmonizes technical skills with mindfulness and intentionality, leading to both personal and professional fulfillment.

To begin crafting this philosophy, reflect on the core principles discussed in this book. Identify which aspects of Zen resonate most with you personally and professionally. Consider mindfulness—the practice of being fully present. How can this deepen your engagement with your code? Develop habits that help you pause, breathe, and reconnect with the task at hand before diving into complex problems. Perhaps incorporating regular reflective moments in your coding routine could align with the Zen principle of introspection, cultivating a practice that fosters continuous growth.

Simplicity is another key principle to embed in your coding philosophy. Emphasize the importance of clarity in code design. Strive for clean, maintainable code that communicates its purpose effectively, ensuring that those who will interact with it can easily understand its logic. How can you challenge yourself to simplify complex implementations? Embrace an iterative approach, regularly reviewing and refactoring code to enhance readability and elegance, akin to honing the precision of each shot aimed toward the target.

Compassion is equally vital. Extend empathy toward the users who will engage with your applications. Prioritize user experience in your designs; understanding their needs will allow you to create solutions that genuinely resonate. Additionally, foster a culture of collaboration within your teams. Recognize the power of supporting one another, encouraging open dialogue and constructive feedback, resulting in a more enriched coding environment for everyone.

The practice of self-reflection and continuous learning should be vital components of your personal philosophy. Commit to analyzing your experiences regularly. What have you learned from successes, and how have challenges shaped your growth? Set clear, articulate goals for learning new languages, frameworks, or methodologies, and embrace the journey of acquiring new skills. Recognize that the coding world is ever-evolving, and maintaining a mindset committed to growth is essential for staying current and resilient.

To prepare for future coding journeys, allow your philosophy to serve as your compass. When faced with challenges—whether a coding crisis, integration hurdles, or the introduction of a new technology—draw upon the principles you have nurtured. Stay mindful in your approach, revisiting the tools and techniques that resonate with you. Reflect on your motivations, ensuring that your coding practice remains aligned with your core values. As obstacles arise, remember to embrace each as an opportunity for growth, leveraging your Zen philosophy to navigate the surrounding complexities with grace.

Finally, take time to celebrate your achievements. Recognize the milestones reached throughout your coding journey, both big and small. Whether it's completing a challenging project, successfully learning a new language, or contributing insightfully to team discussions, honor these moments and the progress you've made. This celebration reinforces the value of your efforts and serves as motivation to strive for further growth, forging an ongoing commitment to the Zen practices you've integrated into your coding philosophy.

In summary, crafting your personal Zen coding philosophy encompasses mindfulness, simplicity, compassion, self-reflection, and a commitment to continuous learning. By embedding these principles into your practice, you create a meaningful framework that not only nurtures technical prowess but also fosters personal growth and resilience. Embrace this philosophy as you navigate your coding journey, letting the wisdom of Zen archer guide you to hit your targets with precision and fulfillment. Through this connection to both your craft and the human experience, your coding practice becomes a powerful expression of clarity, creativity, and purpose.

As you prepare for future coding journeys, carry these insights with you. Allow your personal philosophy to shape your approach, navigating challenges with the calm confidence of a Zen archer. Celebrate each achievement and recognize the profound impact your work can have. With this mindful commitment to your craft, the path ahead will be illuminated by intention and grace.

As you celebrate your achievements, honor not only the milestones reached but also the progress made along the way. Acknowledge the hard work, resilience, and dedication that have brought you to this point. Recognizing and celebrating growth reinforces motivation and ensures the journey continues with clarity and purpose. The commitment to your craft as a coder intertwines with the principles of Zen, as you navigate this journey with mindfulness, creativity, and compassion. Embrace the spirit of the Zen archer as you continue to hone your skills and strike true with every coding endeavor.

15.4. Preparing for Future Coding Journeys

Preparing for future coding journeys necessitates an intentional consideration of the principles and techniques that you have cultivated throughout this exploration of Zen, archery, and coding with Emacs. As the journey continues beyond the pages of this book, it becomes evident that the skills you've acquired extend beyond mere technical proficiency—they also encompass the mindfulness, reflection, and growth that embody the spirit of the Zen archer aiming for the bullseye.

To effectively prepare for the challenges that lie ahead, start by solidifying your coding philosophy. Reflect on the key principles discussed in this book, such as mindfulness, simplicity, compassion, and continuous learning. Consider how each of these can serve as guiding lights in your coding practice. Create a personal manifesto, outlining how you will embody these principles in your future projects. This written tone will become a valuable touchstone to refer back to, reaffirming your commitment to a mindful and intentional approach as you navigate the ever-changing landscape of technology.

Next, set specific long-term goals for your coding journey. Just as an archer defines objectives related to accuracy, distance, and skill development, you should outline your aspirations in the realms of coding languages, frameworks, and methodologies. Consider creating a roadmap with defined milestones that reflect your interests, whether it's mastering a particular programming language, contributing to open-source projects, or participating in tech conferences. This roadmap will provide direction and purpose, helping you stay engaged in your professional growth.

Incorporating reflection into your coding practice is paramount. At the end of each significant project or coding session, dedicate time to reflect on your experiences. Ask yourself: What went well? What lessons did I learn? How can this inform my future practices? This reflective practice reinforces your knowledge, drawing connections between experiences and insights, and shaping your understanding as you make future decisions in your coding endeavors.

Engage with the broader coding community to expand your network and gain insights into emerging technologies. Participate in online forums, attend meetups, and collaborate on open-source projects. These connections not only nurture relationships with other coders but also expose you to diverse perspectives and practices—each contributing to your growth and adaptability as a coder. Embrace the spirit of collaboration and support within these communities, allowing you to share knowledge and inspire one another on the road to continued mastery.

As you prepare for the uncertainties and pressures that often accompany coding projects, remind yourself of the resilience and adaptability embodied in Zen philosophy. Embrace change as a teacher rather than an obstacle. Let go of the fear or anxiety associated with unexpected disruptions, and instead, approach these moments with curiosity and willingness to learn. Maintain a flexible mindset that allows you to pivot when necessary, adapting your practices to accommodate new information or changing project requirements.

Finally, cultivate a sense of balance in your coding journey. Recognize the importance of self-care and personal well-being in your growth as a coder. Consistently prioritizing mental health and nurturing your personal fulfillment allows you to sustain motivation and creativity in your coding practice. Non-coding activities such as spending time with loved ones, pursuing hobbies, or engaging in mindfulness practices can recharge your spirit and keep you grounded amidst the rigors of programming.

In conclusion, preparing for your future coding journeys embraces the integration of Zen principles drawn from your experiences within "The Zen Archer's Emacs." By solidifying your philosophy, setting purposeful goals, engaging in reflection, connecting with the community, embracing change, and prioritizing balance, you embark on an ongoing path of mastery and mindfulness in your craft. As you navigate the vast landscape of technology, allow these guiding principles to steer you on your journey, ensuring each coding endeavor resonates with clarity and purpose.

Celebrating your achievements reinforces the essence of this journey. Take time to reflect on the progress made throughout your coding experiences. Recognize both the seed of knowledge planted through challenges faced and the fruits of labor harvested in the form of completed projects, learning milestones, and personal growth. Allow this celebration to serve as a motivation to continue pursuing excellence, grounded in gratitude and appreciation for your path as a coder.

As you move forward, remember the spirit of the Zen archer and the mindfulness that guides your practice. Embrace new challenges and opportunities, knowing that each experience contributes to your mastery. With each line of code, each thoughtful interaction, and each mindful practice, you continue to hit the bullseye in your coding journey, with clarity and precision as your true aim.

15.5. Celebrating Your Achievements

In the journey of coding within the Emacs environment, celebrating your achievements is not merely an act of recognizing completed tasks; it embodies a vital practice of reflection, appreciation, and motivation that fuels your ongoing development as a coder. Just as a Zen archer takes time to honor their shots—both successful and those that miss—the act of celebrating your coding accomplishments fosters a deeper connection to your craft, enhances your personal growth, and cultivates a spirit of gratitude for the journey you've undertaken.

Begin by acknowledging both the large milestones and the small victories along your path. Each completed project, refactored section of code, or resolved bug represents a step forward in your coding journey. Reflect on the effort, creativity, and dedication that went into achieving these tasks, and take a moment to appreciate your hard work. This act of recognition is essential; it embodies the essence of the Zen practice where mindfulness extends beyond the moment of creation to encompass the journey as a whole.

Document your achievements as you go. Maintain a coding journal or a digital log where you can list the specific outcomes you've completed, insights gained, and impacts made through your work. Whether it's a feature you implemented, a programming language you mastered, or a helpful contribution to an open-source project, keeping track of your accomplishments offers a tangible reminder of your progress. Revisiting these entries serves to reinforce a sense of continuity in your journey, reminding you of the strides you've made and the growth you've experienced along the way.

Incorporate the practice of sharing your achievements with others. Celebrate your successes within your coding community, whether through online forums, team meetings, or professional networks. Sharing not only allows you to express gratitude but also invites encouragement and collaboration from peers who may resonate with your experiences. Much like an archer who may share their techniques and insights with fellow practitioners, open discussions about accomplishments foster a community spirit that helps everyone grow.

Take the time to acknowledge the challenges you faced and overcame to reach your achievements. This reflection deepens your appreciation for the journey, as it reinforces the realization that progress often necessitates hard work and resilience. Instead of viewing setbacks solely through the lens of frustration, you can transform them into learning opportunities that propel you forward. Celebrate not just the successful outcomes but the growth that arose from navigating obstacles, understanding that it is often through struggle that valuable lessons emerge.

As you celebrate these moments, cultivate an attitude of gratitude that extends beyond your personal achievements. Acknowledge the resources, support from peers, educational materials, and experiences that have contributed to your journey. This generous recognition affirms the interconnectedness of the coding community and reinforces a culture of collaboration. Fellow coders, mentors, and communities play an invaluable role in shaping your practice, and celebrating this support generations more strength and motivation.

Establish rituals for celebrating your achievements that resonate with you. These could be as simple as taking time for reflection at the end of each project, sharing your successes with friends or colleagues, or setting aside time to engage in a personal endeavor that brings you joy. Such rituals create a sense of significance around achievements, tuning your mind to appreciate the fruits of your labor while reinforcing your motivation for future coding endeavors.

Lastly, use the momentum generated from celebrations as fuel for your next challenges. Allow achievements to bolster your confidence and enthusiasm, demonstrating that you are capable of facing complex problems and mastering new skills. Setting forward-looking goals based on past successes helps maintain the natural flow of your momentum. Just as an archer builds upon previous shots to refine their aim, coders can harness the knowledge and insights gained from their accomplishments to tackle new projects and push their boundaries further.

In conclusion, celebrating your achievements transcends the act of acknowledging completed tasks; it represents a vital aspect of personal and professional growth in your coding journey. By reflecting on accomplishments, documenting progress, sharing successes, acknowledging challenges, cultivating gratitude, establishing rituals, and using momentum for future endeavors, you embody the principles of Zen as you navigate the world of coding. Embrace this practice wholeheartedly—celebrate each line of code, each resolved challenge, and each connection made in your journey to hit the coding bullseye with clarity and purpose. As you honor your growth, you're not only recognizing your achievements but also propelling yourself forward into a future rich with transformative possibilities.

www.ingramcontent.com/pod-product-compliance
Lightning Source LLC
LaVergne TN
LVHW051332050326
832903LV00031B/3494